Valley Collection . . .

Gorge Connection

Kathy Eastman • *Cheryl Laurance*

Printed in the Columbia
Gorge with recycled paper

5th printing 1992

Printed in the United States of America

For additional copies, please write to:

> *Valley Collection...Gorge Connection*
> *P. O. Box 275*
> *Hood River, Or   97031*

Library of Congress Catalog Card Number 70-82327

ISBN -0-9621252-0-2

Published by Kathy Eastman
                    Valley Collection Cookbooks

Table of Contents

Just a Note. . .

We created _Valley Collection. . . Gorge Connection_ because of our desire to share recipes from our kitchen and those of other Columbia Gorge residents, restaurants, and inns. After months of laughter and tears, WE DID IT!

This book is a sampling from many local people and other friends from across the continent, who for years have shared their love of cooking with us. Some recipes are family favorites handed down from generation to generation, while others have been passed from friend to friend--the original source long since forgotten. Equally outstanding are the original creations contributed by friends, chefs and inn-keepers whose recipes appear on these pages. All have been tested for quality and edited for clarity and consistency.

Enjoy your taste tour of the area's finest recipes from grand hotels, wineries, family inns and restaurants, as well as from community members, and create their specialties at home with this collection.

Dedicated to our husbands and children who so lovingly took over in our homes and especially the kitchen, while we created our cookbook... and for always being there!

Special Thanks. . .

When we first developed the idea to create *Valley Collection. . .Gorge Connection*, we thought the two of us would solely be responsible for all aspects of making it a reality. Yet, it could not have been possible without the behind-the-scenes support of a superlative group of people to whom we would like to extend a special thanks.

PEGGY DILLS KELTER, ARTISAN, who designed and created our cover and indexed pages which so beautifully complement the text.

ALICIA VIK, who donated her computer and patience and whose perseverance and guidance helped take this book from a dream to reality.

DAVE CUNNINGHAM and CLAIRE HASER, MT. HOOD EXECUTIVE SERVICES, who patiently struggled through educating us in the computer world, and who donated many hours toward the cookbook and turned over their office space to us many times.

SYDNEY BLAINE, ELLEN LARSEN, DOROTHY LAURANCE, ERIK EASTMAN, ROD LAURANCE, our friends and family members who offered an ever-present enthusiasm, encouragement, and support. They deserve a special award for the many hours spent working with us. They were a continuing inspiration!

MIMI MACHT, a wonderful friend who gave so generously of her time and whose technical and moral support are so greatly appreciated.

BETTY REA and HELEN VIK, last, but certainly not least, our mothers, for providing us through the years with the inspiration, love and joy for cooking.

ii

**A special thank you goes to the following, for
allowing us to feature a sampling of their recipes.**

Andrew's Pizza & Bakery
Bingen Bakery
Bridal Veil Franciscan Villa
Charles Hooper Family Winery
Clubhouse
Coffee Spot
Columbia Gorge Hotel
Dobré Deli
Eve Atkins Distilling Company
Fruit Tree
Flying L Ranch
Grand Old House
Hood River Hotel
Hood River Village Resort
Inn of the White Salmon
Llama Ranch Bed and Breakfast
Mio Amore Pensione
Mt. Hood Fruit Company
Mt. Hood Railroad
Multnomah Falls Lodge
Old Theater Mercantile & PieBirds Café
Orchard Hill Inn
Rio Grande Mexican Restaurante
River Bend Country Store
Scholls Ferry Farms
Stonehedge Inn at Wildwood Acres
Three Rivers Winery
Timberline Lodge
Williams House Inn
Wine Sellers
Wy'East Naturals
Yaya's International Café

Thank you, thank you, thank you...friends and family members, who so willingly contributed their favorite recipes for our cookbook.

Irene Aikin
Arlene Allegre
Wendy Anderson
Bev Armitage
Leonard Aubert
Ruth Babson
Debbie Bayer
Helen Bellinger
Bette Benjamin
Sydney Blaine
Ann Costello
Joella Dethman
Eloise Dunn
Bug Eastman
Erik Eastman
Erin Eastman
Bev Elsner
Bea Fischer
Sharon Fitzsimmons
Lillian Foster
Mavis Frederickson
Jackie Frost
Jeanne Gaulke
Marilyn Goldsmith
Bob Gosslee
Gayle Gray
Maryann Hanners
Claire Haser
Sandra Haynie
Sandy Henderson
Jennifer Hill
Lee Hollomon
Anne Holman
Marilyn Hopson
Bessie Huck
Marian Hukari
Cindy Janney
Catherine Kelter
Peggy Dills Kelter
Myrna Kemper

Dede Killeen
Linda Klindt
Dorothy LaRue
Ellen Larsen
Sara Larson
Ina Lassen
Dorothy Laurance
Heather Laurance
Nic Laurance
Robin Laurance
Rod Laurance
Shelley Lax
Karen Louiselle
Monsignon John Lunney
Joan Lynch
Mimi Macht
Cheryl Madsen
Larry Madsen
Shirley Mallon
Gloria Mathews
Mary Mauroni
Ruth McAlexander
Pat McDonald
Jan Merz
Kate Mills
Mary Moore
Nona Moore
Kathy Oates
Jennifer Price
Aileen Pobanz
Betty Rea
Pam Riedl
Charlene Rivers
Leona Rosentreter
Randy Salter
Mary Schlick
Becky Schmuck
Lois Sharkey
Christie Smith
Helen Claire Smith

Marilyn Smith
Kitsy Stanley
Doris Suriano
Azusa Suzuki
AnnSwain
Jan Tatyrek
Phillis Temple
Tom Temple
Jannie Tollerud
Jean Tollerud
Helen Vik
JoAnn von Lubken
Dorothy VonderBecke
Max Wahl
Grace Wenger
Chris Weseman
Virginia Wheeler
Myrtle White
Shirley Williams
Georgine Winn
Laura Young

Because this section of the Northwest has so many
spectacular places in which to picnic and hike, we felt it
appropriate to name some of the recipes after favorite local
destinations. It truly is the Gorge and Valley for all seasons.
The following index includes those locations mentioned in
the cookbook.

Appetizers

Maryann's Champagne Punch

1 bottle champagne
1 bottle Sauternes
1/4 cup brandy

Mix together and enjoy!

Maryann Hanners, Hood River

Margarita Punch

1 small can frozen undiluted concentrated limeade
1 small can frozen undiluted concentrated
    lemonade
1 can tequila
1/3 cup Grand Marnier*
2 bottles club soda

ice cubes or molded ice ring

Combine all ingredients in punchbowl and stir with a wire whisk until all frozen juice is dissolved.

Serve cold in salt-rimmed glasses.

*May substitute frozen concentrated orange juice

Punch Bowl Fruit Punch

1 large can frozen orange juice
2 large cans frozen lemonade
1 can fruit blend juice
1 can frozen raspberry juice

2 to 3 liters club soda or to taste

Mix first four ingredients together. You may freeze a small portion of this in a decorative mold for your punchbowl. When ready to use, mix one to two quarts of concentrate with one to two liters of club soda.

Punch Bowl Falls is a beautiful spot that shouldn't be missed. A short hike from Eagle Creek Campground takes you to overnight and day use facilities.

Fruit Punch

6 cups boiling water
4 cups sugar or 3 cups honey
1 large can pineapple juice
2 cups orange juice concentrate
2 lemons
5 ripe bananas, mashed
club soda or 7-up

Make a syrup with the water and sugar. Allow it to cool. Combine the pineapple juice, orange juice, juice from the lemons, and the syrup. Add the mashed bananas. This is your concentrate and can be frozen for later use. Makes about 4 quarts concentrate. Freeze some in a mold for punch bowl.

When ready to use, mix each quart concentrate with one large bottle club soda.

This can be made up a week before and frozen. The mixture is excellent frozen as popsicles.

Hot Clam Dip in French Bread

16 ounces cream cheese
2 cans minced clams with juice
1/2 tsp. salt
juice from one lemon
5 green onions, chopped
1/2 tsp. dill
1 Tb. parsley
1 unsliced round French bread

Mix cream cheese, clams, salt, lemon juice, onions, dill and parsley. Cut off top of bread and pull out bread in chunks, leaving some bread near crust. Reserve these chunks of bread in plastic to use for dipping.

Put cheese mixture in scooped out bread. Put top back on and wrap tightly in foil.

Bake at 225° for 2-1/2 to 3 hours. Unwrap bread and place on platter to be served with reserved, bite-size chunks of bread.

The crust can be pulled apart and eaten when dip is almost gone.

The Wine Sellers

The Wine Sellers, an exceptional wine shop,
is located in the historic Ezra Smith house at
514 State Street, Hood River.

*Let Don and Catherine Kelter help you choose a
perfect bottle of local, regional, or imported wine.
Available to you by the glass, bottle or case.*

*The Flour Garden Bakery keeps fresh-baked
baguettes on hand to complement the many
specialty cheeses and gourmet items offered by
The Wine Sellers.*

*Visit Monday through Saturday for a light lunch in
a friendly atmosphere. While you are there, ask
to be on their mailing list for information on the
up-coming monthly complimentary wine-tastings.*

Microwave Fondue

This fondue as prepared at The Wine Sellers is an easy adaptation of an old favorite.

For each serving:
3 ounces of cheese, grated
    (half Gruyere, half domestic Swiss)
1 Tb. flour
garlic salt
1/2 cup dry white wine
nutmeg

French bread chunks or apple slices

Into a small glass bowl, toss cheese with flour and add a pinch of garlic salt. Add the wine and a shake of nutmeg.

Cover and microwave* on high heat for 3 minutes. Stir and microwave uncovered for 1 minute more.

* These microwave directions are for a carousel-type model. With a "stationary" model, it may be necessary to stir several more times.

Recipe offered by Catherine Kelter, The Wine Sellers.

Panorama Point
Phyllo Triangles

makes 40 appetizers

spinach pie filling, page 112
1 pound frozen phyllo leaves, thawed*
butter

Prepare filling according to recipe's instruction. Cut phyllo leaves lengthwise into 4 equal strips. Cover with waxed paper, then with damp towel to keep them from drying out. Using 2 layers of phyllo at a time, brush butter on one strip. Place 1 rounded tablespoon filling on one end of strip; fold end over end (like a flag), into a triangular shape, to opposite end. Brush entire triange with butter. Place on ungreased cookie sheet. Repeat with remaining strips and filling.**

Bake at 375° for 16 to 20 minutes, or until puffed and golden.

*To thaw: place unopened package in refrigerator overnight. Sheets will handle best if thawed in this fashion.

**To do ahead: cover tightly with plastic wrap at this point and refrigerate no longer than 6 hours. Otherwise, you may cook, cool, cover and refrigerate no longer than 24 hours. To serve, heat for 10 minutes at 350°.

From Panorama Point, there is a spectacular view of the Hood River Valley and Mt. Hood. Take Hwy. 35 just 1/4 mile south of Hood River, then follow Eastside Road 2-1/2 miles to the viewpoint. A beautiful sight any season of the year.

Spicy Avocado Vegetable Dip

1 egg
2 Tb. lemon juice
2 Tb. Dijon mustard
white pepper
1/2 cup salad oil

1 avocado
2 Tb. onion, cut
1/2 cup plain yogurt
1/2 tsp. cumin
dash tabasco
salt

Place egg, lemon juice, Dijon and white pepper in a food processor or blender. With machine on, slowly pour in 1/2 cup oil through tube to make mayonnaise.

Add avocado and onion and purée until smooth. Add yogurt, cumin and tabasco. Blend and season to taste.

Serve with jicama, baby corn and other traditional dipping vegetables.

Lee Hollomon, Silverton

Nut Cracker Dip

1 8 ounce package cream cheese
1/4 cup smoked almonds, chopped
1/2 cup mayonnaise
5 slices bacon, cooked and crumbled
1 Tb. chopped green onion
1/2 tsp. dill weed
1/8 tsp. pepper

Mix ingredients together. Excellent served with crackers, vegetables or gourmet chips.

JoAnn von Lubken, Hood River

Hot Artichoke Dip

1 ounce jar marinated artichoke hearts,
*   drained and chopped*
1 cup mayonnaise
1 cup freshly grated Parmesan cheese
8 ounces cream cheese, optional
paprika

Combine chopped artichoke hearts, mayonnaise, Parmesan cheese, and cream cheese. Heat through. Transfer to fondue pot or chafing dish to keep warm. Sprinkle with paprika.

Serve warm with crackers, rounds of French bread, or try our favorite choice, bread sticks.

Spinach Dip

1 package Knorrs vegetable soup mix
1 package frozen chopped spinach, drained
1 cup sour cream
1 cup mayonnaise
8 ounces cream cheese, softened
Worcestershire sauce
grated onion

Combine the above ingredients together and mix well. Chill.

Serve with carrot sticks, celery, cucumbers, and jicama.

This is wonderful served in a scooped-out squash, cabbage, or small pumpkin.

Harvest Apple Dip

8 ounces cream cheese, softened
1/2 cup vanilla yogurt
1/4 tsp. cinnamon
1/2 tsp. ginger
1 Tb. lemon juice
2 Tb. brown sugar
1/2 cup shredded apple

Combine cream cheese and yogurt, mixing well. Add remaining ingredients. Refrigerate if not using immediately.

Apple dip is great served with celery, apple wedges and carrot sticks, but best of all, kids love it! For a decorative touch, serve in a scooped out large apple.

Debbie Bayer, Fairbanks, Alaska

The Hood River Valley has vast orchard land and is home of world-famous Hood River winter pears and apples. Other delectable valley fruits include cherries, berries, peaches, and both wine and fruit grapes.

The Hood River Valley Scenic Route tour takes visitors through a variety of orchards where each season brings a different focus to the trees, with Mt. Hood as its majestic guardian.

Kate's Salmon Log

2 cups cooked and flaked salmon
8 ounces cream cheese, softened
1 Tb. lemon juice
2 tsp. A-1 sauce
1 tsp. Worcestershire sauce
1/4 tsp. each salt and pepper
1/4 tsp. liquid smoke
dash of Tabasco

1/2 cup chopped walnuts
3 Tb. chopped parsley

Combine the first 8 ingredients. Mix and chill until firm. Shape into 2 logs or balls and roll in the chopped nuts and parsley. Refrigerate. They may be wrapped in foil and frozen at this point.

Serve with crackers.

Kate Mills, Mt. Hood

Mt. Hood School House - 1914, Mt. Hood Towne Hall

This building served as a schoolhouse for pioneer settlers who came to the Hood River Valley in the early 1900's. Originally built as a one room log schoolhouse, the builing was located at a popular Indian camping site on the trail over Mt. Hood. The school was later rebuilt and enlarged as more families moved into the area. From its beginning, the building has served as a community center for many activities. Today the old schoolhouse fills the need for Mt. Hood citizens as a social gathering place, and it houses many of the area's country fairs and quilt shows.

Easy Cheese Ball

12 ounces cream cheese
1/3 cup Parmesan cheese
1/4 cup mayonnaise
1/4 tsp. garlic salt
1/8 tsp. oregano
finely chopped walnuts

Blend all ingredients in a mixer. Shape into 3 or 4 balls and roll in chopped walnuts. Refrigerate. Can be frozen for later use.

Jennifer Hill, Parkdale

Pineapple Cheese Ball

2 8 ounce packages cream cheese, softened
1 small can crushed pineapple, drained
seasoning salt, to taste
1/3 cup onion, finely chopped
1/4 cup green pepper, finely chopped
1-1/2 cups walnuts or pecans, finely chopped

Combine all ingredients, reserving 1 cup of the nuts. Mix well. Form into a ball. Put remaining walnuts on foil and roll ball in nuts. Shake off excess. Refrigerate. Serve with assorted crackers.

Robin Laurance, Parkdale

Tempting Shrimp Spread

1/4 cup butter, softened
1 8 ounce package cream cheese, softened
2 tsp. mayonnaise
dash of garlic salt
1/8 tsp. pepper
1/8 tsp. Worcestershire sauce
2 tsp. lemon juice
1 small onion, finely chopped
1/2 cup celery, finely chopped
2 4-1/2 ounce cans small shrimp, drained
    (or 1/2 pound fresh)

crackers or party rye bread

Combine butter, cream cheese, mayonnaise, garlic salt,
pepper, Worcestershire sauce, and lemon juice. Mix well.
Stir in onion, celery, and shrimp.

Serve with crackers or party rye bread.

Pat McDonald, Hood River

Smoked Salmon Spread

8 ounces cream cheese
1/2 cup sour cream*
1 Tb. fresh lemon juice
1/4 pound smoked salmon, chopped fine
2 Tb. fresh chives, finely minced
pinch of cayenne pepper

Combine all ingredients. Use immediately or refrigerate until
ready to use.

Serve with fine wafers, gourmet chips, or vegetables.

*Can be thinned with more sour cream and used as a dip, if
desired.

Dobré Deli *opened in 1977, with Jan Minarik offering wonderful specialty coffees, desserts, croissants, frozen yogurt and substantial and unusual sandwiches. Located on a shady, tree-lined street in the heart of downtown The Dalles, Dobré Deli also offers catering, from weddings to whitewater trips, box lunches, and of course, lunches to go.*

The soups and salads are made on the premises and may be enjoyed with a variety of beers and Northwest wines.

Outside tables in a backyard setting are available to those who enjoy the warmth The Dalles and Dobré Deli offer.

Dobré Deli Shish-Kebabs

A catering favorite!

Cut into 1-inch squares a light cheese, such as Monterey Jack or Mozzarella cheese, and marinate in Italian dressing 2 to 12 hours. Alternate cubes on frilled toothpicks with cubes of turkey, black and green olives, cherry tomatoes, and salami squares, three to a toothpick.

Stick toothpicks into pumpkin, gourd, or halved grapefruit, cut side down.

Recipe offered by Jan Minarik, Dobré Deli.

13

Egg Roll Appetizers

1 package Won Ton wrappers

1-1/2 cups shredded cooked chicken
1 8 ounce can water chestnuts, chopped
1/2 small onion, chopped
1 cup celery, chopped
1 Tb. soy sauce
2 Tb. cornstarch
1 tsp. ground or freshly grated ginger
1/2 tsp. garlic salt

Dip:
2/3 cup catsup
1/4 cup coarse ground horseradish

Mix all ingredients. Place one heaping teaspoon of mixture on center of wrapper. Fold in two opposite corners, then fold third corner and roll toward the fourth corner. (Resembles a small spring roll).

Moisten the fourth corner with water and seal. Fry in 1 to 2 inches of oil at 350° for about 1 minute or until browned; you may fry several at a time. Serve with dip.

Charlene Rivers, Parkdale

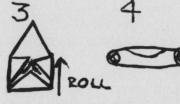

Tilly Jane Puff Pastry

2 puff pastry sheets
4 Tb. sweet, hot mustard
1/2 pound thinly sliced deli ham or turkey
1/4 pound sliced Swiss cheese
1 egg, beaten with 1 Tb. cream

Place 1 puff pastry sheet on cookie sheet. Spread 2 Tb. mustard to within 1 inch of edge on bottom pastry sheet. Layer the meat and cheese on top of the mustard. Top with remaining 2 Tb. mustard.

Fold up the sides and brush with cold water. Trim 1 inch off edge of second puff pastry sheet. Place second sheet directly on top of filling, so that the pastry top will adhere to the edges of the bottom crust. Press edges together with a fork.

Chill for 1 hour. Brush with egg wash. Bake at 450° for 16 to 20 minutes until pastry has puffed and is lightly brown. Make sure bottom crust is done. Cool slightly before cutting into 1-1/2 inch squares.

This is best when eaten freshly baked.

Tilly Jane Forest Camp, in its spectacular setting, is located near the base of Cooper Spur. The camp is a starting point to the Timberline Trail around Mt. Hood and the Mt. Hood Wilderness. A short walk from the campground takes you above the timberline to a magnificent close-up view of Mt. Hood. The easily traveled gravel road is some-times not open until July because of its high elevation.

Brie in Brioche

2 cups flour
2 tsp. baking powder
1 tsp. salt
1/2 tsp. dry mustard
2/3 cup shortening
1/2 cup boiling water
1 Tb. lemon juice
1 egg yolk

1 2-1/2 pound round Brie cheese
1/4 cup chopped green onions

1 egg yolk
1 Tb. water

Mix flour, baking powder, salt and dry mustard. Stir into the
flour mixture, the shortening, boiling water, lemon juice, and
1 egg yolk. Cover and refrigerate pastry until chilled, about
30 minutes.

Divide pastry into halves. Roll one half into a 14- inch circle
on a lightly floured board. Place circle on an ungreased
cookie sheet. Remove paper from Brie, leaving outer
coating intact. Place Brie on center of pastry. Sprinkle
green onions over cheese. Bring pastry up and over
cheese. Press pastry to make smooth and even; trim if
necessary.

Beat 1 egg yolk with 1 Tb. water; brush over top edge of
pastry.

Divide remaining pastry into halves. On a lightly floured
board, roll one half into a 9-inch circle; trim evenly to a
8-1/2-inch circle. Place on top of Brie without stretching
pastry. Press with fingers to make a tight seal.

Roll remaining pastry out. Cut out decorative flowers and leaves for top of brioche. Brush pastry with egg yolk mixture. Arrange leaves and flowers around edge and on center of pastry circle. Brush leaves and flowers lightly with egg yolk mixture. Freeze uncovered no longer than 24 hours.

Bake frozen Brie at 425° until golden brown, 30 to 35 minutes, watching carefully! Cool on cookie sheet on wire rack about 1 hour. Place on serving plate while warm. Cut into wedges to serve.

Refrigerate any leftovers and reheat wrapped in aluminum foil at 350° for 20 minutes.

Chile Cheese Squares

1/4 cup butter
10 eggs, beaten
1/2 cup flour
1 tsp. baking powder
dash salt
1 8 ounce can chopped green chiles
2 cups creamed cottage cheese

1 pound Monterey Jack cheese, grated

Melt butter in a 9x13-inch baking dish. Set aside. Combine eggs, butter, flour, baking powder, salt, chiles, and cottage cheese together. Mix until well blended.

Pour into pan and top with grated cheese. Bake at 400° for 15 minutes, reduce heat to 350° and cook for an additional 30 minutes. Cut in 1-inch squares. Serve warm or at room temperature.

Artichoke Nibblers

2 6 ounce jars marinated artichoke hearts
1 small onion, finely chopped
1 clove garlic, minced
4 eggs, beaten
1/4 cup seasoned fine bread crumbs
1/2 tsp. salt
1/8 tsp. _each_ pepper, oregano and Tabasco
1/2 pound sharp Cheddar cheese*, grated
2 Tb. minced parsley

Drain marinade from one jar of the artichokes. Sauté onion
and garlic in marinade for about 5 minutes. Drain other jar
and chop all the artichoke hearts.

Beat eggs, crumbs, salt, pepper, oregano and Tabasco. Stir
together the cheese, parsley and artichoke/onion mixture.
Turn into a greased 7x11-inch baking dish. Bake at 350° for
30 minutes. Cool 2 hours and cut into 1- inch squares.
Warm before serving.

*For a sharper flavor, use 1/4 pound Cheddar, 1/4 pound
  hot pepper cheese.

A favorite of Kathy's mom, Betty Rea

Crab Stuffed Mushrooms

24 to 30 large mushrooms
1 cup Italian dressing

1-1/2 cups crab, fresh or canned
1/2 cup bread crumbs, plus 2 Tb.
2/3 cup mayonnaise
1 egg, beaten
1 Tb. lemon juice
salt

Wash mushrooms and remove stems. Marinate for at least 2 hours in Italian dressing.

Combine crab, 1/2 cup bread crumbs, mayonnaise, egg and lemon juice. Mix well and add salt to taste.

Remove mushrooms from refrigerator and lay hollow side up in a 9x13-inch baking pan. Mound about 1 Tb. crab mixture in each cap. Sprinkle with remaining 2 Tb. bread crumbs. Bake at 350° for about 20 minutes. Serve hot.

Pesto Stuffed Mushrooms

butter
mushrooms, washed and stems removed*
pesto**
Parmesan cheese, grated

Melt enough butter to just cover the bottom of a 9x13-inch
baking pan. Lay mushrooms in pan. Fill each mushroom
with enough pesto to reach the top of the hollowed cap.
Sprinkle with Parmesan. Bake at 325° for about 15 minutes
or until mushrooms are hot through and start to soften.

* You may use as many mushrooms as you like as there are
no rules in this recipe!

**Pesto may be purchased at The Coffee Spot, Wy'East
Naturals or in the deli section of most supermarkets. You
may also refer to the recipe for Cheese and Pesto
Sandwich.

*When buying mushrooms that will be stuffed, choose ones
with creamy white caps and closed bases. Save the stems
after removing to make stock or mushroom soup!*

Florentine Mushrooms

12 ounces Italian sausage
1 pound spinach, or 1 box frozen, thawed and
    drained
1 tsp. dried dill weed
1-1/2 cups shredded Monterey Jack or Gruyére
    cheese
1/2 cup ricotta cheese
24 to 30 large mushrooms
1/4 cup melted butter

Crumble sausage and fry in a large skillet. Cook over medium
heat until sausage is well browned. Drain sausage, saving
1 Tb. of drippings in pan. If using fresh spinach, add to frying
pan w ith 2 Tb. water and cook until limp, about 2 minutes.
Drain and chop. Combine spinach with sausage, dill and
cheeses.

To prepare mushrooms, wash and remove stems. Place
butter in a 9x13-inch baking dish. Add mushrooms, turning to
coat. With mushroom cavity side up, mound filling in center.
Bake uncovered at 350° for 20 minutes or until hot
throughout. Serve warm. May be kept warm in a low oven.

Anne's Japanese
Chicken Wings

3 pounds chicken wings, tips removed
1 beaten egg
1 cup flour
1 cup butter

Cut wings in half. Dip in beaten egg and then in flour. Fry in butter until brown and crisp. Put in shallow roasting pan and pour sauce over wings.

Sauce:
3 Tb. soy sauce
3 Tb. water
1 cup sugar
1/2 cup vinegar
1/2 tsp. salt

Bake at 350° for 1/2 hour. Spoon sauce over wings during baking.

Anne Holman, Lumsden, Canada

Cocktail Swedish Meatballs

1 cup fine bread crumbs (3 slices bread)
1 pound ground beef
1/2 pound ground pork
1 egg
salt and pepper
1/4 tsp. allspice
1/4 tsp. nutmeg
1/2 cup chopped onion
1/2 cup half-and-half
1/4 cup finely chopped parsley

Mix ingredients together and form into 1-inch balls.

3 Tb. butter
2 Tb. flour
1 cup beef broth
1 cup half-and-half

Heat butter in skillet and brown meatballs, shaking pan while cooking. Remove the meatballs from the skillet and add flour to pan. Heat until mixture bubbles. Add the half-and-half and broth. Stir until blended. Return meatballs to sauce. Simmer 30 minutes.

Helen Vik, Anchorage, Alaska

23

Parmesan Rice Balls

makes 3 dozen

1/2 cup long grain rice
1 10 ounce package frozen chopped spinach,
*   thawed and squeezed dry*
1/4 cup grated Parmesan cheese
1 Tb. lemon juice
1/2 tsp. salt
1/4 tsp. pepper
3 eggs
1 Tb. water
3/4 cup dried Italian bread crumbs
salad oil

Prepare rice according to package directions, or use 1-1/2 cups cooked rice.

In medium bowl mix rice, spinach, Parmesan cheese, lemon juice, salt, pepper and 2 eggs. Shape into 1-inch balls.

In pie plate beat 1 egg with water. Place bread crumbs on wax paper. Dip rice balls in egg mixture, then into bread crumbs to coat evenly.

Fry rice balls in about 3/4- inch salad oil (350°) until golden brown. Drain on a paper towel. Serve warm.

Salmon Nuggets

1/2 cups freshly cooked or canned salmon
1/2 cup mashed potatoes
1 Tb. minced celery
1 Tb. minced onion
1 Tb. butter
1/2 tsp. salt
pepper to taste
1 tsp. Worcestershire sauce
1/2 pound Cheddar cheese, cut in 1/2-inch cubes
1 cup bread crumbs (may use Italian)
1 egg, beaten

Remove all hard bones and skin from salmon and mix well with mashed potatoes. Sauté the celery and onion in butter until tender. Mix with salmon. Add seasonings and shape into balls the size of walnuts. Put a cube of cheese in the center of each ball and reshape. Roll in beaten egg, then in crumbs and fry in enough oil to cover, at 375° for 2 to 3 minutes. Remove before the cheese pops open. Drain on paper towel. May be kept warm in low oven. Serve warm.

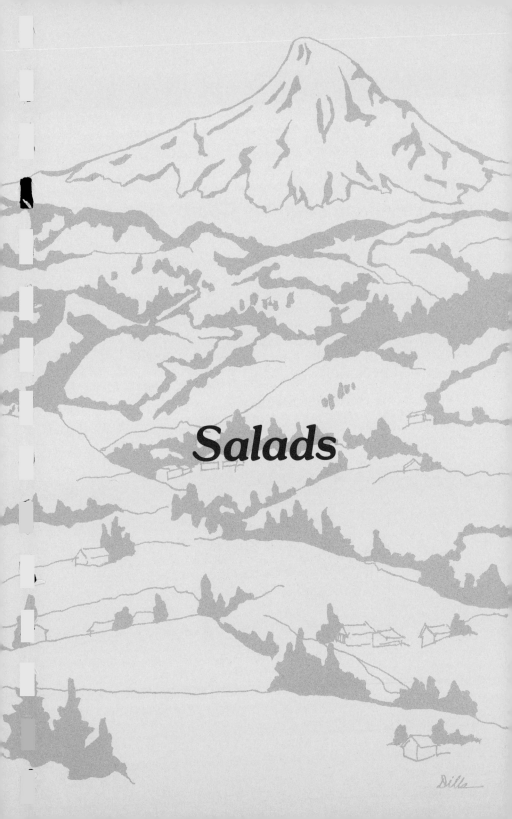

Salads

Eve Atkins Distilling Company

The Eve Atkins Distillery, located a few miles south of Hood River on Summit Drive, is a family-owned and run business. In the tasting room, visitors are invited to sample the various eaux de vie, spirits which have been distilled from the juice of fresh, ripe apples, pears, cherries, blueberries and marion blackberries. Whether used as a dessert brandy, or as an ingredient in haute cuisine, the essence of each particular fruit is preserved in the rich, clear liquid of the Marichelle brandies.

Marichelle

Hood River Salmon Roll

1 fresh salmon fillet, roughly 16 by 4 inches
2 Hood River green apples
1 lemon, juiced
1 Tb. fresh horseradish, finely grated
4 ounces cream cheese
3 Tbs. whipping cream
1 tsp. salt
1/2 tsp. pepper
2 Tbs. sugar
2 Tbs. herbs (finely chopped dill, parsley and
                chives)
1 1/2 ounces Marichelle Apple Eau de Vie

Cut 4 inch squares from a fresh salmon fillet with a sharp knife, salt, pepper and set aside. Coarsely grate both apples and marinate for 1/2 hour in the lemon juice, sugar, horseradish and Eau de Vie. Set aside 1/2 of the apple marinade.

Combine the cream cheese, whipping cream, salt, pepper and chopped herbs with the remaining half of the marinade, stirring until smooth, and cover the salmon squares 1/4 inch deep with the mixture.

Roll the salmon squares tightly and cut each in half with a sharp knife. Serve the stuffed salmon rolls on a bed of bite-size pieces of leaf lettuce which has been covered with the remaining half of the marinade.

Recipe offered by Klaus Trebes, Gargantua Restaurant, Frankfurt, Germany

Columbia Gorge Hotel

Perched high above the Columbia River, *The Columbia Gorge Hotel offers a pleasant return to the Roaring Twenties and a true dining experience. The Columbia Court Dining room specializes in Pacific Northwest cuisine- a unique blend of Nouvelle and classic European cuisine with food from the rich soils and mighty rivers of the Pacific Northwest. Emphasizing in fine dining and a wine list of over 300 selections, Chef David Graignic has become one of the Pacific Northwest's premier chefs.*

Chef Graignic learned his craft by working with several of the leading chefs in the Northwest. After 6 years at the Columbia Gorge Hotel, he has created his own distinct style by blending traditional recipes with his own, specializing in imaginative light sauces and use of herbs grown on the hotel grounds.

The Columbia Gorge Hotel serves a world-famous farm breakfast every day, featuring apple blossom honey 'from the sky' on hot, freshly baked biscuits, fresh fruits, oatmeal, meats, potatoes, eggs and pancakes.

Sacajawea, the Indian wife of Lewis and Clark's French-Canadian interpreter and the legendary heroine of the expedition, was chosen to symbolize the Columbia Gorge Hotel's generosity and devotion to quality.

Warm Spinach Salad with Smoked Duck

serves 2

5 bunches spinach
1 breast of smoked duck, cut in strips
1 hard boiled egg, chopped fine
4 Tb. crisp bacon, crumbled
2 Tb. Cognac

Dressing:
1 Tb. dry mustard
2 Tb. Worcestershire sauce
1/8 cup sugar
1 cup olive oil
1/2 cup red wine vinegar

Wash spinach and break into large pieces. Set aside. Mix all ingredients together for dressing. Simmer until warm with the bacon and smoked duck. Pour only the dressing over salad and toss. Reheat the duck and bacon again, flame with 2 Tb. Cognac and toss with spinach to wilt. Sprinkle chopped eggs on top. Toss gently and serve.

Offered by the Columbia Gorge Hotel.

28

Greek Salad

serves 8

1/3 cup olive oil
1/4 cup red wine vinegar
1 tsp. cracked black pepper
1 tsp. basil
2 Tb. chopped parsley
1/2 tsp. oregano
1/4 tsp. salt

2 bunches romaine lettuce, torn into bite-size pieces
3/4 cup Feta cheese, crumbled
sliced tomatoes
sliced cucumbers
Greek olives

Make dressing by combining oil, vinegar, oregano, parsley,
salt and pepper in a jar and shake well. Toss dressing
with the torn lettuce leaves. Add crumbled cheese, olives,
tomatoes and cucumbers; lightly toss. Serve on cold salad plates.

Cobb Salad

serves 4

1 large head iceberg lettuce
1 bunch watercress, optional
1 cup shredded cooked chicken breast, optional
3 hard boiled eggs, chopped
2 Tb. crumbled bacon
1/3 cup crumbled Bleu cheese
4 medium tomatoes, chopped
2 medium avocados, chopped
1 cup diced Cheddar cheese
3 Tb. chopped green onions

Italian dressing

Shred lettuce and put in bottom of salad bowl. If using watercress, chop.

In individual rows on top of lettuce, place the chicken, eggs, bacon, Bleu cheese, tomatoes, avocados, cheese and green onion. Cover with plastic wrap and chill. Just before serving, toss with salad dressing.

Enjoy!

This is a beautifully colorful salad. A complete meal in itself with freshly baked croissants or sourdough bread, soup, or a great addition to a barbecue (in which case, you may choose to omit the chicken).

Spinach Salad with Chicken & Berry Vinegar

serves 2

1 bunch spinach, washed and torn
1 whole chicken breast, skinned, boned and
  pounded flat
flour seasoned with salt and pepper, for dredging
1 Tb. butter
2 Tb. good quality olive oil
1 Tb. minced shallots, or 2 tsp. minced garlic if
  shallots are unavailable
3/8 cup blackberry or raspberry vinegar, recipe
  follows
2 tsp. lemon juice (omit if using raspberry
  vinegar, which is already tart)
1/2 cup cubed Swiss cheese
1/4 cup toasted walnuts, coarsely chopped
1/2 cup sliced mushrooms

Prepare spinach and place on dinner plates. Dredge
prepared chicken breasts with flour. Heat butter and olive oil
in a skillet over low heat. Add shallots and saute until soft but
not brown, on both sides. Remove breast and cut in
bite-sized piece. Do not clean pan. Add berry vinegar to
shallot /oil drippings and deglaze pan. Allow vinegar to
thicken slightly by simmering. Return chicken to pan and
finish cooking in vinegar sauce, for a few minutes. Add
lemon juice. There should be enough sauce at this point to
dress your salads. If not, add a bit more vinegar. Remove
chicken with sauce from pan and place on spinach, pouring
sauce over all. Add Swiss cheese, mushrooms and garnish
with walnuts. Serve with French bread from the *Wine
Sellers*.

A Zinfandel or Pinot Noir is a lovely wine to serve with this.

Peggy Dills Kelter, Hood River

31

Oregon Berry Vinegar

Gather 4 pounds fresh blackberries or raspberries. (Make sure to pick berries that do not grow along busy roads--for your health!) Sort fruit and remove any moldy berries, and leaves. Rinse fruit and drain in colander. Transfer berries to a gallon glass jar (with rust proof top) and crush fruit using hands or a potato masher. Add 1 quart distilled white vinegar. Cover tightly and store in a cool dark place (the basement works well) for 3 to 4 weeks, stirring every few days.

Line a large bowl with an old pillowcase or scrap of muslin. Pour in the fruit/vinegar mixture. Gather up the cloth and tie with a string. Hang this dripping ball over the bowl overnight, or until the vinegar stops dripping. Don't squeeze.

Discard drained fruit. Measure rendered vinegar. For every 2 cups vinegar, measure 3 Tb. sugar. Heat sugar in a low oven (300°) for 8 minutes. Pour vinegar into a wide pot so the vinegar is no more than 4-inches deep. This will expedite boiling process, keeping the beautiful color intact. Place vinegar over high heat and warm. Stir in warmed sugar and bring quickly to a boil. Boil
3 minutes. Pour into a clean container and let stand until cool.

Bottle in clear bottles so that everyone can admire the beautiful color. Do not bottle every last drop as you will end up with sediment. Cork or seal tightly and store in a cool dark place.

Peggy Dills Kelter, Hood River

Chicken Sesame Salad

serves 4

s
a
l
a
d

3 to 4 cups shredded cooked chicken breasts

2 Tb. sesame seeds
4 Tb. lemon juice
1/4 cup salad oil
1-1/2 Tb. white wine vinegar
2 cloves minced garlic
1-1/2 Tb. soy sauce
2 tsp. finely minced ginger
1/2 pound Chinese pea pods (snow peas)
1/2 pound bean sprouts

Toast sesame seeds in a small pan over medium heat until seeds are golden brown. In a large bowl mix the seeds, lemon juice, oil, vinegar, garlic, soy sauce and ginger until combined.

Fill a large pan half full with water; bring to a boil. Add pea pods and bean sprouts and cook just until water returns to a boil. Drain and rinse with cold water and drain again.

Combine chicken, oil mixture, and vegetables. Stir until all ingredients are combined.

This easy to put together salad makes a perfect light summer meal. Great served in pocket bread!

Village Chicken Salad

serves 6 to 8

A perfect cold salad for summer .

4 whole chicken breasts, skin removed
1/2 cup soy sauce
1/2 cup sherry
2 celery stalks with leaves
1-1/2 tsp. sugar
2 cloves garlic, mashed
3/4 cup mayonnaise
1 tsp. sugar
1 tsp. lemon juice
1/2 tsp. soy sauce
1 large bunch broccoli, broken into florets
1/2 cup chopped celery
1/2 cup chopped scallions
1/2 cup unsalted cashews

Combine 1/2 cup soy sauce, sherry, celery, sugar and garlic in a large frying pan. Add chicken breasts and simmer until tender. Slightly cool chicken; bone and cube. Return chicken to cooking liquid until completely cool.

Steam broccoli until crisp tender, about 5 minutes. Cool.

Mix together mayonnaise, sugar, 2 Tb. of the cooking liquid, lemon juice and 1/2 tsp. soy sauce. Drain chicken. Add chicken to mayonnaise dressing.

Toss all with remaining ingredients. Refrigerate several hours or overnight.

Great served with fresh pineapple.

Pam Riedl, Hood River

Chinese Sesame Salad

serves 6

2 whole boneless, skinless chicken breasts,
  cooked and diced into bite-size pieces
1 pound dry noodles or 9 ounces fresh
  (angel hair or spaghetti)
1 bunch green onions, cut in 2-inch lengths,
  and then julienne
3/4 cup coarsely chopped almonds
1 small can sliced water chestnuts
1/2 to 3/4 cup vegetable oil
2 to 3 Tb. sesame oil
2 Tb. sesame seeds
1/2 cup soy sauce
1 Tb. ground coriander

2 to 3 tsp. Chinese hot oil* (or to taste)

Cook noodles according to package directions. Rinse in
cold water and drain well. Toss with chicken,onions,
almonds and water chestnuts. In a small sauce pan over
medium low, heat vegetable oil, sesame oil and sesame
seeds until seeds begin to turn brown. Remove from heat
and stir in soy sauce and coriander (carefully, as it will bubble
up). Cool slightly and stir in Chinese hot oil. Pour over
noodle mixture and toss well to coat. Refrigerate for at least
3 hours before serving. Keeps well.

*Purchase in the Oriental section of most markets. You
may also find sesame oil in this area.

If you have a preference for hot tasting food, this salad may
be hotter in flavor by carefully adding more Chinese hot oil!

Chinese Maifun Salad

serves 4 to 6

2 cups oil
2-1/2 ounces Maifun noodles*
3 dried Shiitake mushrooms*
1 cup cooked, shredded chicken breasts
1 head shredded lettuce
2 green onions, chopped
3 Tb. toasted sesame seeds
1/2 cup toasted slivered almonds

Dressing:
1/4 cup rice vinegar
1/4 cup vegetable oil
1 tsp. sesame oil*
2 Tb. sugar
1/4 tsp. black pepper
1/2 tsp. salt

Heat oil in wok to 400°. Put in 1 Maifun noodle stick. If it puffs up immediately, put in a small handful. Turn rice sticks over to allow the sticks on top to puff. Remove immediately. Set aside.

Soak dry mushrooms in water for 20 minutes. Discard stems and slice mushrooms into thin strips. Prepare dressing.

Have other ingredients cut and ready. Combine all ingredients and toss with dressing just before serving.

These items may be found in the Oriental section of most markets.

Shirley Williams, Odell

Chinese Almond Rice Salad

serves 8

s
a
l
a
d

1/3 cup whole almonds
1 tsp. soy sauce
3 cups cooked long grain rice
1 cup diagonally sliced celery
1 small head Chinese cabbage, thinly sliced
1-1/2 cups shredded cooked chicken breast
1/2 cup chopped green onion

Place almonds on baking pan and sprinkle with 1 tsp. soy sauce. Toast at 300° for 15 minutes, turning frequently.

Combine rice, chicken, celery, onion and 2 cups cabbage. Add dressing and almonds; mix well.

Soy dressing:

1/2 cup oil   *2 Tb. catsup*
2 Tb. vinegar   *1/4 tsp. garlic powder*
2 tsp. brown sugar   *1/4 tsp. ground ginger*
3 Tb. soy sauce

Put all ingredients in a jar and shake well.

Japanese Chicken Salad

serves 6

2 Tb. salad oil
1 package Oriental noodle soup mix,
    no seasoning
1/2 cup sliced almonds
2 Tb. sesame seeds
2 cups shredded or diced cooked chicken breast
4 cups finely shredded green cabbage
1/2 cup chopped green onions
salt

Rice Vinegar Dressing:
1/3 cup salad oil
1/3 cup rice vinegar
5 tsp. sugar
1/2 tsp. pepper

Heat oil in wide frying pan over medium-high heat. Crumble noodles; add to oil with almonds and sesame seeds. Cook, stirring until browned (3 to 4 minutes). Lift out mixture; drain.

In a salad bowl, combine noodle mixture, chicken, cabbage, and onions. Season with salt to taste. Prepare rice vinegar dressing and pour over salad. Mix lightly until well coated.

Myrna's Rice Salad

1 package Almond "Rice-a-Roni"
3 sliced green onions
1 can water chestnuts, drained and chopped
1 6-1/2 ounce jar marinated artichoke hearts
     with marinade, cut in bite-size pieces
1 small can pitted black olives
1/3 cup mayonnaise

Prepare rice according to package directions. Cool. Add green onions, water chestnuts, artichoke hearts with marinade, and olives. Toss with mayonnaise to coat rice. Chill thoroughly. Best if made a day before. Stir just before serving.

Myrna Kemper, Parkdale

Snow Shoe Curry Rice

2 Tb. salad oil
2 Tb. lemon juice
2 Tb. finely chopped onion
1 tsp. salt
pepper
1 tsp. curry powder
1-1/2 cups cooked rice
1-1/2 cups cooked chicken
1 cup chopped celery
3/4 cup mayonnaise
2 Tb. chopped green pepper

Combine oil, lemon juice, onion, salt, pepper and curry powder. Add rice, chicken, celery, green pepper and mayonnaise. Mix well and chill before serving.

Great lunch on a snowy trail! Sydney always doubles this recipe.

Sydney Blaine, Parkdale

Vegetable Rice Salad

2 cups carrots
1/2 cup green onions
1 stalk celery
1 small green pepper
4 cups cooked brown rice, cooled*
1/2 cup sunflower seeds

Thinly slice all vegetables and add to rice and sunflower seeds. Prepare dressing.

Lemon-Basil Dressing:
1/4 cup lemon juice
1/3 cup olive oil
2 cloves garlic, minced or pressed
1 tsp. salt
1-1/2 tsp. dried basil
1/2 tsp. dry mustard
1/2 tsp. sugar
1/4 tsp. pepper

Mix all dressing ingredients together and pour over rice mixture. Cover and chill several hours to blend flavors, stirring occasionally.

To serve, place romaine lettuce on plate or platter. Top with rice mixture. Garnish with sliced tomatoes or alfalfa sprouts.

* 2 cups bulgur wheat soaked in 2-1/2 cups water may be used in place of brown rice. Bulgur should soak until all water is absorbed, about 1-1/2 hours.

Gayle Gray, Parkdale

Ladd Creek Pasta Salad

1 pound spiral noodles
2 large tomatoes, cut up
2 6 ounce jars marinated artichoke hearts, drained
     and chopped
1 green pepper, thinly sliced
3/4 cup chopped onions
5 ounces thinly sliced pepperoni
1 6 ounce can small pitted ripe olives
3 Tb. olive oil
1 Tb. red wine vinegar
1 clove garlic, minced
1/4 cup chopped parsley
2 tsp. salt
1 tsp. basil
1/2 tsp. oregano
1/2 tsp. pepper
8 ounces Feta cheese

Cook pasta according to package directions. Drain. Mix all
remaining ingredients together, except Feta cheese. Mix with
pasta. Chill salad. Add Feta cheese just before serving.

Pam Riedl, Hood River

---

*Ladd Creek Campground is located at the junction of Ladd Creek
and the West Fork of the Hood River. It is a very small campground
and receives only moderate use. Plenty of room for those who like
seclusion.*

Bald Butte Pasta Salad

8 ounces spinach fettuccine, or seashell pasta
1 pound cauliflower florets and/or broccoli florets
2 large carrots, cut into small rounds
2 medium zucchini, cut into 1/4-inch strips
2 sweet red peppers, seeded and cut into slivers
    (may substitute a green pepper)
1 cup frozen green peas, rinsed in hot water
1 medium red onion quartered and sliced thin

Dressing:
1/4 cup minced fresh parsley (or 2 Tb. dried)
1/4 cup fresh basil leaves, minced (or 1 Tb. dried)
1 large clove garlic, crushed
1/4 cup olive or vegetable oil
1/4 cup chicken or vegetable broth
1/4 cup red wine vinegar
4 tsp. Dijon mustard
1/2 tsp. salt, or to taste
freshly ground black pepper

Combine dressing ingredients in a small bowl and mix. While the pasta is cooking, steam the broccoli, cauliflower and carrots until   crisp-tender. Rinse in cold water. In a large bowl combine steamed vegetables with remaining vegetables. Toss well. Pour dressing over the pasta mixture and toss together to combine them well. Chill the salad for 1 hour or longer before serving.

Cooked chicken, pork, slivered beef or seafood may be added to provide main-course protein.

Just like Bald Butte, this salad is beautiful winter or summer.

Compliments of Mary Schlick, Mt. Hood

Shelley's Salmon Salad

2-1/2 cups pasta, rotini or bows
1 7 ounce can salmon*
1-1/4 cup chopped cucumber
1 cup plain yogurt
1/4 cup mayonnaise
2 Tb. chopped green onion
1 tsp. dried dillweed
1/2 tsp. salt, optional

Cook pasta according to directions on package. Drain and cool. Combine pasta, seafood and cucumber.

Mix together yogurt, mayonnaise, onion, dill and salt. Pour over pasta mixture. Toss lightly to coat.

Chill 1 hour to blend flavors.

* You may substitute salmon with tuna, shrimp, crab, or fresh seafood.

Shelley Lax, Lumsden

_____

Elaborate fish ladders are found at Bonneville Dam, which are used to preserve the valuable runs of migrating fish. Visitors can watch the fish through underwater windows at the Bonneville Visitors Center. The project is 40 miles east of Portland in the heart of the Cascades.

43

Columbia Pasta Shrimp Salad

1/4 cup white wine vinegar
3 Tb. lemon juice
1-1/2 Tb. honey
1 Tb. chopped fresh ginger
1 Tb. soy sauce
3 dashes cayenne pepper
1-1/2 pounds large shrimp
12 ounces favorite pasta   (curly, fettuccine, penne)
1 Tb. Oriental sesame oil
1 bunch green onions, chopped
1 tsp. sesame seeds
grated peel of one lemon

In a 4 quart saucepan, stir together first 7 ingredients. Bring to a boil over high heat, stirring once or twice; cover and remove from heat. Let stand for about 10 minutes, covered, until shrimp is done. Cut to test. Shrimp should be opaque. Remove shrimp from liquid and refrigerate; reserve liquid.

Meanwhile, cook pasta according to package directions. When done, rinse with cold water and drain.

Combine cooked pasta, reserved liquid, shrimp, oil, onions, lemon peel and sesame seeds until blended well. May be made up to one day ahead. Chill and serve.

This is a perfect salad to bring along on a picnic with a loaf of French bread and sparkling cider. Enjoy while watching the windsurfers sail the Columbia!

Savory Mustard Mousse

s
a
l
a
d

4 eggs
1 cup water
1/2 cup vinegar
3/4 cup sugar
1 envelope unflavored gelatin
1/2 tsp. tumeric
1-1/4 tsp. dry mustard
1/4 tsp. salt
1/2 pint heavy cream

Beat eggs in the top of a double boiler. Add water and vinegar. Mix sugar, gelatin, mustard, tumeric and salt together. Add to egg/vinegar mixture. Cook over boiling water, stirring constantly until thick. This may take some time. Cool. Whip cream and fold into gelatin mixture.

Pour into mold and refrigerate until set. Garnish with parsley on a bed of lettuce.

Marilyn enjoyed this served at a Christmas buffet with ham. Also wonderful in the summertime as a cool, light accompaniment to cold smoked ham.

Marilyn Hopson, Lumsden,Canada

Marinated Vegetable Platter

1 bunch broccoli
1 to 2 heads cauliflower
2 baskets cherry tomatoes
4 carrots, cut in small strips
1 bunch chopped green onions
3 stalks celery
1/2 pound mushrooms
2 cans pitted black olives, drained
2 cans artichoke hearts, drained
12-ounce bottle Italian dressing

Prepare all vegetables, cutting into bite-size pieces. Cherry tomatoes should be left whole. Put all ingredients in a plastic sealable bag. Marinate and refrigerate for 24 hours turning frequently. Drain thoroughly before serving on a platter.

This is wonderful as a buffet salad!

Marinated Tomatoes

1/2 pound mushrooms, sliced
3 Tb. chopped green onions
5 large tomatoes, sliced

Marinade:
1 tsp. curry
1 tsp. sugar
1/2 cup salad oil
1/4 cup vinegar
1 clove garlic, minced
1 Tb. parsley
salt and pepper

Combine all marinade ingredients together. Pour over vegetables and marinate for at least 6 hours in the refrigerator. To serve, arrange on a bed of lettuce.

Light Yogurt Potato Salad

serves 8

s
a
l
a
d

2 pounds red potatoes
1/2 cup plain yogurt
1/2 cup mayonnaise
3 Tb. rice wine vinegar
2 cloves minced garlic
2 tsp. thyme leaves, crumbled
1/4 to 1/2 cup sliced green onions
1/2 cup thinly sliced celery
salt and pepper to taste
parsley for garnish

Boil potatoes until tender, about 20 minutes. Drain and cool.
Cut into bite- size cubes. Combine yogurt, mayonnaise,
vinegar, garlic, thyme, onions and celery. Mix dressing
gently into potatoes. Season with salt and pepper. May be
made 24 hours ahead. Cover and refrigerate.

Walla Walla Potato Salad

serves 12

3 pounds red new potatoes
1 large Walla Walla Sweet onion
1 cup thinly sliced celery
1 large Golden Delicious apple
12 green olives, sliced
1/2 cup chopped sweet pickle
1-1/2 cups mayonnaise
1 tsp. Dijon mustard
1 Tb. vinegar
2 Tb. soy sauce
salt and pepper to taste

In pan place potatoes in 1 inch of boiling water. Cover and steam until tender. Drain and cool. Dice potatoes and put them in a large bowl. Cut onion in quarters and slice thin. Add to potatoes along with the celery, apple, olives and pickles. Stir together mayonnaise, mustard, vinegar and soy sauce. Spoon over potatoes and mix gently. Season with salt and pepper. Refrigerate for 2 hours or overnight.

Cauliflower and Kidney Bean Salad

A wonderful garlic-lover's salad!

s
a
l
a
d

1 large head cauliflower (8 cups)
2 15-1/4 ounce cans good quality kidney beans,
    drained, reserving 6 Tb. liquid
1 cup mayonnaise
2 cloves garlic, pressed or minced

Core the cauliflower and separate into 1/2 to 3/4-inch florets. Stalks can be cut up small and included if there are not enough florets. Mix cauliflower and beans in large bowl.

In a separate bowl, mix together mayonnaise, garlic and reserved bean liquid until smooth. Pour mayonnaise over cauliflower/bean mixture. Mix, cover and refrigerate. Chill at least 2 to 12 hours, 24 hours is best. Serve cold.

Claire Haser, Mt. Hood

Overnight Broccoli Cauliflower Salad

serves 8

1 head broccoli
1 head cauliflower
1 cup frozen tiny green peas
1 cup sour cream
2 cups mayonnaise
 garlic salt to taste
1 tsp. lemon juice
1 bunch green onions, chopped

Wash broccoli and cauliflower and break into small pieces. Mix all ingredients together. Cover and chill overnight.

Cooking at the end of the day comes easy when this do-ahead salad is served with a steak cooked on the grill.

49

Dog River Cilantro Salad

4 cups cooked black-eyed peas, or 2 cans
    Trappey's Black-eyed peas with jalepeño
    peppers
3 cups cooked and cooled white or brown rice

Salsa:
1 small white onion, finely chopped
2 large tomatoes, chopped
2 small cucumbers, peeled and chopped
1 bunch fresh cilantro, washed and chopped*
1 to 5 jalapeño peppers, seeded and diced*
salt and pepper

If using dried peas, cook according to package directions.
Cool. If using canned, drain. Combine peas with cooked rice.

Prepare next 5 ingredients and mix together. Add peppers
according to taste intensity desired. You may also add a bit of
cilantro and peppers to bean/rice mixture if you choose.

On a serving platter, make a ring of bean/rice mixture creating
a well in the center.

Spoon the salsa in the center and garnish with additional
sprigs of cilantro or parsley if desired. Refrigerate until cold.

*Available in most grocery store produce departments .

*An excellent but easy salad for the Mexican flavor lover. Great
as a meal in itself or as a complement to grilled steak.*

Dede Killeen, Parkdale

Bea's Cole Slaw

serves 4 to 5

s
a
l
a
d

1 tsp. salt
1/4 tsp. pepper
1/2 tsp. dry mustard
1 tsp. celery seed
2 Tb. sugar
1/4 cup chopped green pepper
1 Tb. chopped red pepper or pimentos ·
1/2 tsp. grated onion
3 Tb. olive oil
1/3 cup vinegar
4 cups chopped cabbage

Place ingredients in large bowl in order given. Mix well.
Cover and chill thoroughly.

Bea Fischer, Mt. Hood

Gazpacho Salad

1 cucumber, sliced
1 red onion, sliced
1 large bell pepper, sliced
2 to 3 tomatoes, sliced

Marinade:
1/4 cup salad oil
1/4 cup red wine vinegar
1/4 cup tomato sauce
salt and pepper

Add marinade to vegetables and refrigerate for 12 hours or
longer.

Serve on a bed of lettuce.

Beacon Rock Three Beans

3 cups cooked small red beans
3 cups cooked black beans
3 cups cooked small white beans

Dressing:
1 cup extra-virgin olive oil
1/4 cup fresh lemon juice
2-1/2 tsp. cumin
1-1/4 tsp. oregano
4 cloves, minced
1 Tb. hot chile oil

1 cup fresh parsley, finely chopped
1/2 cup fresh cilantro, finely minced
1/3 cup fresh mint, finely minced
salt and freshly cracked black pepper to taste

Combine ingredients for dressing. Toss with beans. Add parsley, cilantro, and mint. Let sit for an hour and then add salt and pepper.

This salad is served at room temperature.

_____

Beacon Rock, an 800 -foot high volcanic remnant, named by Lewis and Clark in 1804, is a notable landmark among the pinnacles and promontories of the Gorge. Beacon Rock State Park provides a picnic area, campsites, and hiking trails to waterfalls, Mt. Hamilton and to the top of Beacon Rock. You can view herons and other birdlife on nearby Pierce Island. This area is sacred to the Indians, and is a land of beauty for all to enjoy.

Hood River Waldorf Salad

serves 4 to 6

2 cups cored and chopped Red Delicious apples
1 Tb. lemon juice
2 cups chopped celery
1 cup chopped walnuts
1/2 cup Salad Mayonnaise, page 60
lettuce leaves

In a large bowl, combine the celery, apples and lemon juice.
Mix well. Add the walnuts and mayonnaise, stirring until
combined. Chill. When ready to serve, spoon the salad into
lettuce-lined bowls.

===============

*Since the Nathaniel Coe Family established the first land
claim in 1854, the population of Hood River Valley has grown
at a steady pace.*

*On February 19, 1895, the city of Hood River was officially
incorporated. By the year 1900 the population was 622, and
within 5 years increased to 1,751 residents.*

*Over a 40 year period the fruit and timber industry, the
Columbia River Highway, the Hood River to White Salmon
Bridge and the Mt. Hood Loop Highway, all played a part in
establishing the present identity and diversity of the Hood
River Valley.*

*The discovery of Hood River as a world-class windsurfing
site in the mid-80's has added a new dimension to the
economy.*

Frozen Apple Salad

1 8-1/2 ounce can crushed pineapple
     (drain and reserve juice)
2 eggs, slightly beaten
1/2 cup sugar
1/8 tsp. salt
1/4 cup lemon juice

2 cups unpeeled, chopped apples
1/2 cup chopped celery
1 cup heavy cream, whipped
1/2 cup chopped nuts

Add water to reserved pineapple juice to make 1/2 cup. In
saucepan combine pineapple juice, eggs, sugar, salt and
lemon juice. Cook over medium heat, stirring frequently
until thick*. Cool in refrigerator. When cool, fold in remaining
ingredients. Spoon into an 8-inch square pan. Cover and
freeze. Allow about 1 hour to thaw. Cut into squares and
serve on lettuce leaves.

*This may take a while to thicken.

Marian Hukari, Parkdale

Dressings

Bev's Rum Dressing
for Fruit Salad

3/4 cup firmly packed brown sugar
1 tsp. dry mustard
1/4 tsp. salt
1/3 cup lime juice
1-1/2 Tb. rum
1 cup salad oil

Combine all ingredients except oil in blender or food
processor. Blend well. While blending, slowly add oil.
Chill.

Delicious as a dip for fruit slices or as a dressing on fruit salad.

Bev Elsner, Husum

Poppy Seed Dressing

makes 1 cup

1/3 cup red wine vinegar
1/3 cup oil
1/4 cup honey
4 tsp. minced onion
4 tsp. poppy seeds
3/4 tsp. mace

Combine ingredients. Cover and refrigerate up to 2 weeks.

*This dressing is lovely served as a dip for fresh strawberries
and melon.*

Green Salad Dressing

1 cup salad oil
1/3 cup catsup
1/2 cup vinegar
1 tsp. Worcestershire sauce
1/2 tsp. salt
1/2 onion, finely chopped
1 clove garlic, minced

Combine all ingredients in an electric blender. Chill.

Left Bank Salad Dressing

makes 1 quart

3 cups salad oil
1 cup mayonnaise
1/2 cup Dijon mustard
1/2 cup red wine vinegar
salt and pepper

Mix all ingredients together and refrigerate.

Offered by Kathy's mom, Betty Rea

Mustard Vinaigrette Dressing

2 Tb. hot mustard
1 Tb. red wine vinegar
freshly ground black pepper to taste
3/4 cup extra virgin olive oil
1 clove garlic, pressed or minced

Blend vinegar, mustard, black pepper and garlic with wire whisk. Gradually add oil while continuing to whisk briefly until oil has been completely blended with vinegar mixture.

d
r
e
s
s
i
n
g

Parmesan Dressing

makes 1-1/4 cups

1 cup salad oil
1/3 cup red wine vinegar
2 Tb. grated Parmesan cheese
1-1/2 tsp. Worcestershire sauce
1/2 tsp. prepared hot mustard
1 tsp. salt
1/4 tsp. each, coarsely ground fresh black
   pepper, paprika and parsley
1/8 tsp. garlic salt

Mix all ingredients together thoroughly. Let stand for at least one hour before using. Refrigerate.

Seafood Louie Dressing

1 cup mayonnaise
1/2 cup catsup
2 Tb. horseradish
dash cayenne
1 Tb. brandy
dash Worcestershire sauce
2 Tb. minced onion
white wine vinegar
juice of 1 lemon
1 cup heavy cream

Combine all ingredients. Chill.

This is a wonderful dressing to compliment your fresh seafood salad.

Cucumber Dressing

1 cup sour cream
1/2 cup grated cucumber
1/2 tsp. salt
1 tsp. dill
2 tsp. chives
1/2 tsp. black pepper

Mix all ingredients together and chill. Excellent on salmon.

Buttermilk Farm Dressing

makes 1 cup

1/2 cup fresh parsley leaves
1/4 cup fresh dill, coarsely chopped
1 green onion, sliced
1 clove garlic, chopped
salt to taste
2/3 cup buttermilk
2 Tb. vegetable oil
freshly ground black pepper

Place parsley, dill, onion, garlic, and salt in a food processor or blender and mix until finely chopped. Add buttermilk and oil and mix until thoroughly blended. Add pepper to taste. Refrigerate overnight.

Serve over green salad, chicken salad or try it on a cold pasta salad. This dressing is very versatile.

Classic Bleu Cheese Dressing

1/2 cup mayonnaise
1/2 cup sour cream, or yogurt
1/2 cup crumbled Bleu cheese
1 Tb. chopped fresh parsley or chives

Mix all ingredients together thoroughly. Spoon over salad greens and offer generous amounts of freshly ground black pepper.

dressing

59

Salad Mayonnaise

makes 1 cup

1 large egg, room temperature
5 tsp. fresh lemon juice
1 tsp. Dijon mustard
1/4 tsp. salt
1/4 tsp. white pepper
1 cup vegetable oil

In a food processor or blender, on high speed, blend the
eggs, lemon juice, mustard, salt, and white pepper. Add the
oil in a slow stream with the processor on. Refrigerate unused
portion.

Cottage Dressing

1/4 cup sugar
1 tsp. salt
1 tsp. dry mustard
1 Tb. onion juice
1/3 cup vinegar
1 cup salad oil
1 Tb. poppyseeds
1-1/2 cups large curd cottage cheese

Mix all ingredients together until well blended. Refrigerate
before serving.

*This is a lovely dressing over a spinach salad, but also works
well with any salad greens.*

Dorothy Laurance, Parkdale

Caper Sauce

Excellent served with fish!

1-1/2 cups mayonnaise
1 tsp. onion, finely minced
2 Tb. parsley, finely chopped
2 Tb. capers
1 tsp. chives, chopped
1 tsp. Dijon mustard
1/2 tsp. tarragon
1 hard boiled egg, chopped
8 anchovy fillets, finely chopped
lemon juice to taste

Mix, chill and let mellow!

Kate Mills, Mt. Hood

Aïoli Sauce

8 garlic cloves, peeled
2 egg yolks
salt and pepper to taste
juice of 1 lemon
1-1/2 tsp. Dijon mustard
1-1/2 cups oil, half olive oil and vegetable, or
        light virgin olive oil (peanut oil may be used)

Have all ingredients at room temperature.

Purée garlic in a food processor or blender. Meanwhile, whisk the egg yolks in a small bowl until smooth. Add to the garlic. Add salt, pepper, lemon juice and mustard and process until smooth. With the machine running, slowly pour in the oil in a slow steady stream. Continue to process until the sauce is thick.

Cover and refrigerate until ready to use.

This sauce is wonderful as a dip for steamed artichokes as well as a tasty sandwich spread!

Ina's Cheese Bread Spread

2 cups grated Monterey Jack cheese
2 cups grated Cheddar cheese
1 cube softened butter
2/3 cup mayonnaise
garlic salt or powder
2 Tb. minced onion
2 Tb. chopped parsley

1 loaf French bread

Mix all ingredients together. Thinly slice a loaf of French bread, or use pre-sliced. Toast bread slices. Spread cheese mixture on one side of bread and broil until cheese is bubbly.

This cheese spread freezes well , so you could always have it on hand for unexpected company.

Ina Lassen, Parkdale

French Herb Butter

1 cup soft butter
4 Tb. soft cream cheese
1-1/2 tsp. minced garlic
1/4 cup chopped fresh parsley*
3 Tb. lemon juice
1 tsp. salt
1/4 tsp. pepper

Beat butter with the cheese until light and fluffy. Beat in remaining ingredients. Cover and refrigerate in the warmest part of the refrigerator.

* In season, you may also use chives.

This is great with crunchy French bread. It can also be used on green beans, pasta or hamburgers.

Recipe offered by Catherine Kelter, The Wine Sellers.

Visiting this quaint country store will give you the feeling that you have stepped back in time to an era of gas lamps and horse-drawn carriages. You'll find antique fixtures beneath a canopy of hanging aromatic herbs and dried flowers. Sample local products from the gourmet selection or the ones made in their own farm kitchen - from corn relish and spiced peaches and apple cider to huckleberry preserves. You may stroll through their river front gardens, nibble a fresh strawberry or try a borage blossom.

Green Tomato Relish

18 cups green tomatoes
2 large onions
1 red pepper
1 green pepper
3 cups vinegar
9 cups sugar
3 Tbs. salt
1 tsp. each: allspice and cloves
2 tsp. each: cinnamon and nutmeg

Grind tomatoes and drain liquid. Grind onions and bell peppers. (It helps to let tomatoes, onions and peppers drain overnight, if possible, to reduce the amount of liquid.) Combine all ingredients and slowly cook, stirring often, until reaching the desired consistency. Pack in sterile jelly jars and seal. Process in hot water bath for 25 minutes.

Delicious when served over hamburger, chicken or scrambled egg.

Offered by River Bend Country Store

63

Entrées

Chicken Breasts in Lemon Cream Sauce

serves 4 to 6

6 chicken breast halves, boneless and skinless
salt and pepper
1/2 cup butter
2 Tb. dry sherry
2 Tb. grated lemon peel
2 Tb. lemon juice
1 cup heavy cream
2 tsp. cornstarch
freshly grated Parmesan cheese

Lightly salt and pepper chicken. Melt butter in heavy skillet and sauté chicken for 8 to 10 minutes, turning once. Place chicken in a 7-1/2 x 11-inch baking dish.

Add sherry, lemon peel and lemon juice to butter in pan. Stir cornstarch into cream and then slowly add to butter and sherry mixture, stirring constantly.

Pour over chicken, sprinkle with Parmesan and broil until golden brown.

Served with a tossed green salad and rice, your guests will think you cooked all day!

Karen Louiselle, Mt. Hood

64

Timberline

Chef Leif Eric Benson, a native of Gotenborg, Sweden, began his apprenticeship at the age of 10 with his father, a chef of 35 years.

He is the current chairman of the Board of the Chefs de Cuisine Society of Oregon and a member of the Northwest Culinary Team that competed in the International Culinary Olympics in Frankfurt, Germany, in 1988.

In the rustic, stone-walled Cascade Dining Room, Chef Benson presents lodge guests and dining patrons with fresh regional dishes with an international flavor, as befits an alpine resort in the fine European tradition.

Timberline Lodge is a unique National Historic Landmark. Explore the lodge and imagine the determination and dream of the men and women who built it.

The lodge has 59 rustic, comfortable rooms, American and continental dining and year round skiing facilities.

Enjoy the feeling of being in a magnificently restored bit of Oregon's history as you experience the spirit of Mt. Hood and the irresistible beauty of Timberline.

Oregon Filbert Chicken Oriental

serves 4

1/3 cup peanut oil
1 pound chicken breasts, boneless, skinless,
  cubed
1/2 cup celery, diagonally sliced
1/2 cup onion, thinly sliced
1/2 cup red and green pepper, thinly sliced
1/2 cup sliced water chestnuts
1/2 cup snow peas

1 cup filberts

Heat the peanut oil over high heat in wok. Add chicken and
stir-fry about 3 minutes, until light brown. Add the
vegetables and nuts, continue to stir-fry for about 3 minutes
more. Add the Oriental Sauce and bring to a boil for about
1 minute.

Oriental Sauce:

1/4 cup cornstarch
1 tsp. garlic powder
1 tsp. ground ginger
1/4 cup rice vinegar
1/4 cup dry sherry
1/3 cup soy sauce
2 cups chicken stock
1/2 tsp. ground black pepper

To make the sauce, combine the dry ingredients and blend
well with the other sauce ingredients.

*This sauce works well on meat, fish and vegetable dishes.
Keep refrigerated.*

Compliments of Chef Leif Eric Benson, Timberline Lodge

entrée

Lime Roasted Chicken

serves 4

3 whole chicken breasts, split
3 to 4 fresh limes
1/4 cup salad oil
1/2 tsp. salt
1/8 tsp. pepper
1 Tb. chopped parsley
1 Tb. capers
2 cooked carrots
2 leeks
3 boiled potatoes, peeled
1/2 pound mushrooms

Place chicken breasts in roasting pan. Juice enough limes to make 1/4 cup. Mix with oil, salt, pepper, parsley and capers. Pour over chicken. Marinate 1 hour.

Bake at 350° for 20 minutes, baste and turn. Add vegetables to pan, basting with marinade. Bake an additional 20 to 30 minutes, until done.

To serve, garnish with lime slices, spooning juices over each individual serving.

Offered by Kathy's mother, Betty Rea

e
n
t
r
é
e

Lolo Pass Chicken Kebabs

boneless, skinless chicken breasts, cut into
*   1-inch cubes*
Italian salad dressing
cherry tomatoes
green and red peppers, cut into 1-inch cubes
mushrooms
pineapple
small white onions

e
n
t
r
é
e

Marinate chicken in dressing and refrigerate overnight. On metal or soaked wooden skewers, slide on cubes of meat, alternating with each vegetable.

Broil or barbecue for 8 to10 minutes, basting with marinade.

==

To journey by car over Lolo Pass, take Dee Hwy to the Lost Lake exit. Travel this scenic area which will eventually reach Brightwood. From this pass you have a close-up view of the west face of Mt. Hood.

68

Honey Glazed Chicken

serves 4

e
n
t
r
é
e

3 to 4 chicken breasts, split, boned and skinned*
1/3 cup flour
1 tsp. garlic salt
1/4 tsp. freshly ground pepper
4 Tb. butter, melted
1/4 cup honey
3 Tb. lemon juice
2 Tb. soy sauce
2 slices minced ginger (about 1 tsp.)

Mix flour, garlic salt, and pepper. Coat chicken thoroughly with flour mixture. Place chicken in a shallow buttered baking dish. Bake at 350° for 20 minutes. Mix sauce of melted butter, honey, lemon juice, soy sauce and ginger.

Pour over chicken. Continue baking, brushing occasionally with sauce for another 20 minutes, until chicken is tender.

*Turkey tenderloin may be substituted.

Herbed Cheese Chicken

serves 6

4 pounds boneless, skinless chicken breasts
8 slices Mozzarella or Provolone cheese,
*   thinly sliced 3x5-inch*
flour
2 eggs beaten, diluted with 3 Tb. water
* seasoned bread crumbs*
1/2 cup melted butter
1 Tb. parsley
1/4 tsp. poultry seasoning
1/4 tsp. basil
1/4 tsp. thyme
1/2 cup sherry

Pound each chicken breast until thin and flat. Season with salt and pepper to taste.

Place a chicken breast on a slice of cheese, roll up and fasten with a toothpick. You may at this time add a thin slice of lean ham to the inside before rolling the chicken up.

Roll each chicken bundle in the flour, egg and breadcrumbs. Melt butter and add herbs. Place chicken rolls in baking pan and drizzle with butter mixture. Bake in a 350° oven for 30 minutes. Pour the sherry over the chicken and bake for 20 more minutes.

This dish is easy yet elegant to serve to company with a Greek Salad and crusty French bread.

Bridal Veil Franciscan Villa

Within the tradition of Franciscan hospitality , the Franciscan Sisters of the Eucharist of Bridal Veil, Oregon, have opened their Villa to meet a variety of needs.

Enjoy a delicious lunch prepared and served by the Sisters. This lovely setting is a unique alternative for business meetings, group gatherings, retreats, seminars or a day of reflection.

Located in the beautiful Columbia Gorge on the Scenic Highway, the Villa sits quietly against the cascading cliffs amongst lush trees and manicured gardens.

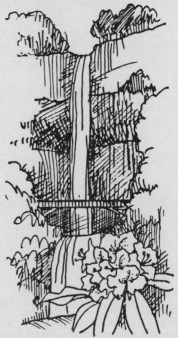

Baked Chicken Breasts in Emerald Barbecue

serves 6

6 chicken breasts, split
1/2 cup flour
1-1/2 tsp. salt
1/8 tsp. black pepper
1 tsp. poultry seasoning
1/2 tsp. paprika
1/4 tsp. granulated garlic
3/4 cup butter, melted

Emerald Barbecue Sauce:
1-1/2 cups dry white wine
1-3/4 cup favorite barbecue sauce

Combine flour, salt, pepper, poultry seasoning, garlic and paprika. Coat chicken with flour mixture.

Dip chicken in melted butter. Place chicken, skin side up, in an open baking pan. Bake uncovered 25 minutes at 400°.

Reduce heat to 325° and continue baking uncovered for 20 minutes. Baste once or twice with natural juices. Baste each piece with Emerald Barbecue Sauce.

To make sauce: simmer wine for 5 minutes. Add barbecue sauce and cook 5 minutes longer.

Serve with Vegetable Rice Pilaf, page 145, for accompanying recipe also contributed by Sister Margaret, and a garden green salad!

Offered by Sister Margaret Boehm, F.S.E., Bridal Veil Franciscan Villa.

entrée

72

Chicken Dijonnaise

serves 4

*3 to 4 chicken breasts, split, boned, skinned and
  cut into strips*
freshly ground black pepper
1-1/4 cup chicken broth
1/3 cup mustard*
1/2 cup butter
1/2 cup vermouth or dry white wine
1/2 cup heavy cream

Brown chicken in butter until lightly cooked. Add pepper,
broth, vermouth, cream and mustard. Reduce heat to low.
Cover and simmer 20 to 25 minutes.

Serve with rice or pasta.

*We like to use 1/2 Dijon and 1/2 coarse Pommery-style
  mustard.

e
n
t
r
é
e

Badger Lake Lemon Chicken

serves 4 to 6

3 whole chicken breasts, boned, skinned and split
1-1/2 cup lemon juice
1 cup flour
1 tsp. salt
1 tsp. paprika
1 tsp. freshly ground black pepper
1/3 cup safflower oil
1-1/2 Tb. grated lemon peel or zest
1/4 cup brown sugar
1/4 cup chicken stock
1 tsp. lemon extract
2 lemons, thinly sliced

e
n
t
r
é
e

Put chicken and lemon juice in bowl or sealable bag and refrigerate overnight, turning occasionally. Drain chicken and pat dry. Combine flour, salt, paprika, and pepper.
Coat chicken thoroughly with flour mixture.

Sauté chicken in oil until lightly browned. Arrange chicken in a shallow baking dish. Sprinkle with lemon zest and brown sugar. Mix chicken stock and lemon extract together and pour around chicken pieces. Put a few slices of lemon on top of each piece of chicken.

Bake at 350° for 30 to 40 minutes. Serve warm or cold.

Chicken Bearnaise

serves 4 to 6

4 whole boneless, skinless chicken breasts
2 tsp. butter
3/4 tsp. salt
dash pepper

e
n
t
r
é
e

In a large skillet, place butter, 1/4- inch of water and salt and pepper. Place the chicken breasts in the pan and bring to a boil. Cover the pan and reduce heat to low. Cook covered for about 15 minutes or until the chicken is cooked through. Remove from the pan with a slotted spoon and place on a platter to keep warm in a low oven. Prepare sauce.

Bearnaise Sauce:
4 egg yolks
1 tsp. instant minced onion
1 tsp. tarragon vinegar
1 tsp. white wine
1/2 cup butter, melted

Place first 4 ingredients in a blender or food processor. Turn to highest speed and gradually add butter mixing well until sauce is creamy and thick.

Pour over chicken breasts and garnish with parsley.

Shirley Mallon, Hood River

Chicken à Latourell Falls

serves 6 to 8

*4 pounds boneless, skinless chicken breasts or
thighs
1/2 cup flour
1 tsp. salt
1/2 tsp. pepper
1/2 tsp. garlic powder
4 Tb. butter
1 to 2 Tb. oil
1 medium onion, sliced
2 leeks, sliced
1/2 pound fresh mushrooms, sliced
1 Tb. chopped parsley
1 cup apple cider*
1 cup heavy cream
1/4 tsp. thyme leaves
1/4 tsp. oregano leaves
1 bay leaf*

e
n
t
r
é
e

Combine flour, salt, pepper and garlic. Dredge chicken
pieces in flour mixture. Melt butter in large skillet and brown
chicken over medium high heat on all sides. Remove from
pan and place in a 9x13-inch baking dish.

To the same pan the chicken was browned in, add 1 to 2 Tb.
oil. Sauté onions, leeks and mushrooms. Stir in remaining
flour, parsley, cider, cream and spices. Cook and stir until
slightly thickened. Pour over chicken. Cover and bake in a
350° oven for 25 minutes. Uncover and bake for 30 minutes
longer or until done.

* May substitute dry white wine for the cider

Debbie Bayer, Fairbanks, Alaska

---

*Latourell Falls is the most westerly of the many cascades in
the Gorge. The trailhead is 2.4 miles east of Crown Point on
the Old Columbia River Highway.*

Chicken Veronique

serves 6

6 halves boneless, skinless chicken breasts
4 Tb. flour, divided
salt and pepper to taste
2 Tb. vegetable oil
1/4 pound mushrooms, sliced
1 cup chicken stock
1 cup heavy cream
1 cup seedless green grapes

Dust chicken in 2 Tb. flour, salt and pepper. Sauté chicken in oil until lightly browned. Add sliced mushrooms and sauté briefly. Add chicken stock and simmer covered for 30 minutes. Remove breasts to serving platter and keep warm.

Mix remaining flour with 1/4 cup water, stirring to make a thin paste. Add to stock and simmer until slightly thickened. Add heavy cream and heat, but do not boil. Add grapes. Pour sauce over chicken pieces and serve immediately.

Linda Klindt, The Dalles

———————————

French canoemen called this place "La Grande Dalle de la Columbia." The same rough rapids were named "The Long Narrows" by Lewis and Clark. Later The Dalles served as a staging area for the Oregon Trail. Today The Dalles is an agricultural center surrounded by cherry orchards and wheat fields.

entrée

77

Chicken Breasts with Capers

serves 4

4 boneless, skinless, chicken breasts
1 Tb. olive oil
1 Tb. butter
2 Tb. capers
3/4 cup white wine
flour
salt and pepper

Coat chicken with flour. Heat olive oil in frying pan. Brown chicken quickly on both sides. Add capers with a little juice and wine. Reduce heat and cook for about 10 minutes. If sauce is too thin, remove chicken and boil it down to a few tablespoons.

Serve each breast with sauce and capers on top.

Phillis Temple, Bend

Rummy Orange Chicken

3 to 4 chicken breasts, boned, skinned and cut in
    2-inch strips
3 Tb. melted butter
1 small can frozen orange juice
1/2 cup rum
salt and pepper
1/2 cup toasted slivered almonds

Arrange chicken in shallow baking dish. Combine butter, orange juice and rum and pour over chicken. Salt and pepper chicken. Bake at 350° for 40 minutes, basting 2 to 3 times during cooking time. Sprinkle on almonds just before serving.

78

Chicken Pesto in Puff Pastry

e
n
t
r
é
e

2 to 3 chicken breasts, boneless, skinless,
    cooked and cooled
4 Tb. pesto*
6 large slices Monterey Jack, Mozzarella, or
    Provolone cheese
6 large slices cooked ham
1 package frozen patty shells
1 egg white
Parmesan cheese
poppy or sesame seeds

Spread pesto over chicken. Wrap a slice of cheese and then ham around each chicken breast. Let patty shell stand at room temperature for 30 minutes, or until thawed. Roll each shell into an 8 to 10- inch circle. Set chicken onto pastry and wrap, pinching seam to seal. Place seam side down on ungreased cookie sheet, brush with egg white. Sprinkle with Parmesan cheese and sesame seeds. Refrigerate for 30 minutes. Bake at 400° for 25 to 35 minutes. Cool 20 minutes before serving.

* May use Dijon mustard with a bit of basil and garlic in place of pesto.

Wonderful for dinner, lunches, or picnics.

Garlic Baked Chicken

3 to 4 chicken breasts, boneless, skinless
1/2 cup lemon juice
1/2 cup olive oil
4 to 6 minced cloves of garlic
1/4 cup Parmesan cheese
1 Tb. pesto or 1/2 tsp. each basil and oregano
freshly ground pepper

Place chicken in shallow glass baking dish with marinade made
from remaining ingredients. Refrigerate 4 hours or overnight,
turning chicken over occasionally to coat. Bake at 350° for 40
minutes, basting twice during cooking time.

*May substitute turkey tenderloin.

wild rice casserole p. 144

Lemon Dill Chicken

serves 3 to 4

2 whole boneless, skinless, chicken breasts
1 Tb. butter
1-1/2 tsp. fresh dill or 1/2 tsp. dillweed
1/4 tsp. freshly ground pepper
1 Tb. lemon juice

Sauté chicken in butter and herbs until tender. Transfer
chicken to serving platter. Add lemon juice to skillet. Heat
through and pour sauce over chicken breasts.

Chicken and Dumplings

e
n
t
r
é
e

3 chicken breasts
2 stalks celery
2 carrots
1 medium onion
parsley
salt and pepper
1 can cream of mushroom soup

Cut vegetables in large chunks. Add chicken, vegetables, and seasonings to 4 to 6 cups water and simmer for 45 minutes, or until chicken is cooked and tender. Remove chicken to platter, reduce liquid to 2 cups and add 1 can cream of mushroom soup. Bring to a boil.

Dumplings:
1 cup flour
2 tsp. baking powder
1/2 tsp. salt
1/2 cup milk
2 Tb. vegetable oil

Mix dumpling ingredients together and drop a tablespoonful at a time directly into boiling stock. Cover lightly and return to a boil. Reduce heat and simmer 12 to 15 minutes. Serve dumplings and gravy over chicken.

Chicken Tetrazzini

serves 6

3 cups cooked chicken*, shredded
1/2 pound pasta**
3/4 pounds mushrooms, sliced
2 to 3 Tb. butter
1 clove garlic
1/2 cup freshly grated Parmesan cheese

Sauce:
3-1/2 Tb. butter
2-1/2 Tb. flour
2-1/2 cups chicken broth
1-1/4 cups heavy cream, heated
4 Tb. dry white wine

Cook pasta according to directions. Drain. Prepare sauce: melt butter and stir in flour. Add chicken broth and heat until slightly thickened. Add cream and wine and heat thoroughly.

Sauté mushrooms and garlic in butter. Remove garlic when mushrooms are limp. Toss with the pasta. Add half the sauce to the chicken and half to the pasta and mushrooms. Place the pasta in a buttered baking dish. Make a well in the center and top with the chicken . Sprinkle with the Parmesan cheese.

Bake at 375° until lightly browned and heated through, about 20 minutes.

*You may substitute cooked turkey for the chicken.
** Twisted, fettuccine, or macaroni may be used.

Ann Costello, Anchorage, Alaska

MIO AMORE PENSIONE

A European Bed & Breakfast Inn

Secluded in beautiful Trout Lake Valley, at the base of Mt. Adams, sits a wonderful surprise for visitors to the great Northwest. **Mio Amore Pensione** *is a European style Bed and Breakfast/Restaurant with an ambiance and warmth to make your stay truly memorable. The owners, Tom and Jill Westbrook, have decorated each of their four rooms with memorabilia from around the world. . . giving each room its own personality.*

If you prefer a more rustic getaway, there is the "Ice-House", a stone building dating back to the 1890's. All rooms come with a full breakfast.

Tom is a gourmet cook and he offers a multitude of epicurean delicacies for your dining pleasure. Your meal will be complemented by one of Jill's desserts, such as Brandy Alexander Pie or Italian Creme Caramel.

Mio Amore offers the perfect year-round getaway, whether you enjoy many of the outdoor activities or simply relaxing by the creek.

Coniglio Arista Alla Vada

serves 4

2-1/2 to 3 pounds fresh rabbit
10 cloves fresh garlic
2 Tb. salt
3 Tb. pepper
3 Tb. fresh rosemary
1/3 cup olive oil
water

entrée

Generously oil a large frying pan with olive oil. Cut rabbit into 1-1/2 to 2 inch pieces. Stuff each with garlic, rosemary, salt and pepper. Place in pan, roll in olive oil. Cover with water.

Bake at 375° for 45 minutes to 1 hour, until water is cooked down. Garnish and serve.

Recipe compliments of Mio Amore Pensione.

Trout Lake is a little-known recreational wonderland surrounded by three wilderness areas: Mt. Adams, Indian Heaven and Goat Rock. The possibilities are unlimited year-round.

Warm weather activities include swimming, tubing, hiking, bicycling, horse-back riding, tennis, back packing, wild berry and mushroom picking, wind surfing, mountain climbing, bird watching, and of course fishing.

In the winter there are just as many activities to occupy one's time, such as cross-country skiing, dog sledding, snowmobiling, ice-skating, and walking.

Not to be overlooked are such activities as the Mayfest in nearby White Salmon, the Huckleberry Festival in Bingen, and the Trout Lake Country Fair.

Mongolian Grill Buffet

serves 6

This is great for a party. Everything can be prepared ahead of time and each guest creates and cooks his /her own stir-fry. Ingredients listed are enough for each guest to have at least 2 servings. Have 2 woks available, if possible, to accommodate more than one cook at once. To simplify self-service at the buffet table, arrange items in order of use. Provide each guest with both a bowl to create in and a separate plate for the final product!

3 pounds thinly sliced beef sirloin, pork, or chicken breasts (or a combination of any, served in separate bowls.

**3 large carrots, thinly sliced on the diagonal
2 stalks celery, thinly sliced on the diagonal
2 large onions, thinly sliced
1/2 pound mushrooms, thinly sliced
1 pound fresh bean sprouts
2 large green peppers, cut into 1/4-inch strips
3 cups shredded Chinese cabbage
1 cup broccoli, cut into small florets**

**dash of hot chili oil*, or more to taste
1/2 tsp. sesame oil*
soy sauce
oyster sauce
rice wine vinegar
sherry or dry white wine
grated fresh ginger root
lemon wedges
minced garlic**

**sesame seeds
vegetable or peanut oil**

Trim any fat from meat and remove all bones. Slice all the meats across grain (easiest if partially frozen) into strips 1/4- inch thick and about 2 to 3 inches long. Refrigerate if done ahead of time.

Refrigerate all the prepared vegetables in separate serving containers.

At serving time, preheat woks or skillets to 350°. For each serving, guests select about 1 cup of mixed vegetables, several slices of meat, and small amounts of each seasoning desired.

Pour 2 tsp. oil into wok and add meat. Cook meat, stirring, for 2 to 4 minutes. Add vegetables and seasoning. Continue cooking, mixing meat with vegetables until vegetables are crisp-tender, about 1 to 2 minutes. Remove to plate and sprinkle with sesame seeds.

Available in the Oriental section of most super markets.

Recipe created by Ellen Larsen, reconstructed from memory of a special dinner out with Mimi, Kathy and Cheryl, prior to a John Denver concert.

entrée

Crown Point Steak

serves 4

4 tenderloin steaks, cut 1-1/2-inch thick
1-2 Tb. green peppercorns
1/8 cup butter
4 Tb. shallots
1/4 cup Cognac
1/4 cup vermouth
2 Tb. Dijon mustard
1/2 cup heavy cream
1/2 cup chicken broth

Sauté steaks in butter until cooked as desired. Remove steaks to warm platter. Sauté shallots. Add Cognac and vermouth, allowing it to flame. Let boil to reduce to a syrup. Add peppercorns, mustard, cream and broth and simmer. Serve sauce over steaks.

Crown Point offers a breath-taking view of the west entrance to the Gorge. From the west proceed on I-84 to the Bridal Veil Exit and follow the signs. Vista House Visitor Center at Crown Point has one of the most photographed views of the Gorge. Built in 1917, it sits high atop Crown Point.

e
n
t
r
é
e

Medallions of Beef with Green Peppercorn Sauce

serves 8

3 pounds beef tenderloin
1 6 ounce can green peppercorns
1/2 cup dry red wine
1/4 tsp. beef bouillon
3 cups heavy cream
1/3 cup brandy
salt to taste

Slice tenderloin into 16 slices. Refrigerate.

In medium saucepan, simmer peppercorns in wine until wine is reduced by half. Add cream and beef bouillon and continue simmering until sauce is thickened and will coat the back of a spoon well. Add salt to taste.

Cook beef medallions, in 2 batches if necessary, in very hot oil (steaks will continue cooking when removed from heat). Remove from pan to a warm place. Deglaze pan by adding brandy and flaming alcohol (alcohol must be cooked out or sauce will be bitter).

Add cream sauce and simmer until blended with steak drippings and is thick enough to coat spoon. Correct seasoning if necessary.

Serve the steaks with a small amount of the sauce and remaining sauce on the side.

Recipe offered by the Columbia Gorge Hotel.

Ginger Beef

1-1/2 pound flank steak (round or top sirloin may be used)

Marinade:
1/4 cup soy sauce
1 tsp. crushed garlic
1 tsp. grated ginger
1 tsp. sugar
1/2 tsp. MSG (optional)

flour
oil

Combine marinade ingredients and stir well. Cut meat in thin diagonal slices and combine with marinade. Marinate meat for 1 hour or more. Flour each piece and fry in oiled skillet.

Azusa Suzuki, Parkdale

Charlene's Beef Roulade

serves 4 to 6

*1-1/2 pounds of thinly sliced sirloin or round
 steak*
Dijon, prepared, and Chinese mustards
pepper
garlic salt
parsley flakes
5 slices of cooked ham, cut in narrow strips
6 carrots, peeled and sliced thin
2 small onion, sliced in 1-1/2-inch lengths
flour
2 Tb. oil
1 cup dry sherry
water

Cut meat into six pieces (4 x 6). Spread thinly with three
mustards. Sprinkle with pepper, garlic salt and parsley. Place
2 to 4 slices of ham, 2 to 4 slices of carrot, and 2 slices of
onion on each piece of meat. Roll up and secure with a
toothpick, making sure all ingredients are tucked inside roll.

Dip in flour and brown in oil in skillet. Reduce heat and
remove meat rolls to baking dish. Add 1 cup sherry to
drippings. Add 1-1/2 cups hot water. Stir to make smooth
sauce. Pour over rolls. Bake 1-1/2 hours at 325°. Sauce can
be thinned or thickened before serving.

Charlene Rivers, Parkdale

entrée

90

Hungarian Stuffed Peppers

serves 8

e
n
t
r
é
e

4 cups canned whole tomatoes, with juice
1 8 ounce can tomato sauce
1 medium onion, finely chopped

6 slices day old bread, cut in 1/2 inch cubes
3 Tb. raw rice
1-1/2 pounds lean ground beef or ground turkey
salt and pepper to taste
8 green peppers, tops removed, seeded and
*   washed*

In a large saucepan or Dutch-oven, place the whole
tomatoes, juice and tomato sauce. Heat.

Soak bread cubes in water for a few minutes, then squeeze
as much moisture out as possible.

Mix together bread, rice, meat, salt and pepper. Spoon
mixture into green peppers.

Place stuffed peppers in tomato sauce. Cover pan and bring
to a boil. Simmer on top of the stove for 1-1/2 hours.

Recipe compliments of Betty Rea.

Mimi's Barbecued Meatballs

serves 6-8

This is a great potluck dish and may be doubled for large crowds .

Meatballs:
3 pounds lean ground beef
2 cups rolled oats
1 medium onion, chopped
1/2 tsp. garlic powder
1 cup milk
2 eggs

Sauce:
16 ounces catsup
1 cup brown sugar
3 tsp. onion flakes or fresh onion
1/2 tsp. garlic salt

Mix meatball ingredients together and form into 1-1/2 to 2-inch balls. Put them into a 9x13-inch baking dish, using an extra pan if needed.

Mix the sauce ingredients together and pour over meatballs. Bake, uncovered, at 350° for 1 hour.

Mimi Macht, Hood River

entrée

The Clubhouse Restaurant

You don't need to be a golfer to enjoy the food and atmosphere at *The Clubhouse.* View the driving range or 9th-hole while feasting on creations of Chef Patrick Edwards. He cooks for you 7 nights a week and the public is invited. The Clubhouse is located at 1850 Country Club Road at the Hood River Golf Course.

Clubhouse Rack of Lamb

serves 6

6 12 to 14 ounce lamb racks
6 Tb. Dijon mustard
1 cup Chapleur
1 pint Sauce Marchant de Vin

93

Chapleur:
1 cup breadcrumbs
1 tsp. *each* chives, parsley and tarragon
1 Tb. garlic, minced

Mix breadcrumbs and herbs together for Chapleur.

Sauce Marchant de Vin:
2 cups beef stock
2 Tb. butter, melted
3 to 4 Tb. flour
2 shallots, minced
1 Tb. butter
1/2 cup red wine

For sauce, thicken beef stock with a roux consisting of melted butter and flour. Add roux to stock, stirring constantly with a whisk. Bring sauce to a slow boil. If sauce is too thick, thin it with more stock or a little red wine. If it is too thin, add a little more roux or cornstarch. This sauce should coat a spoon when dipped into it. Strain sauce into a clean heat-proof container and keep warm in a double boiler or a bath of hot water and cover with a lid.

Sauté shallots in butter until slightly browned and add 1/2 cup dry red wine. It should resemble a thick syrup. Add to sauce and mix. Cover sauce and keep warm until ready to serve.

Ask your butcher to remove the fatty cap from the lamb racks and French- trim the meat from between the ribs, about 1 to 2 inches from the top or just down to the eye of the rack.

Season the racks with salt and pepper and brown on all sides in a skillet on medium-high heat. Arrange them on a roasting pan with ribs standing up. Spread Dijon mustard over the eye of the racks and top lightly with the Chapleur.

Bake at 425° for 20 to 30 minutes. Lamb is usually served medium-rare to medium.

Serve rack of lamb in a pool of Sauce Marchant de Vin, along with vegetables, potatoes, or rice of your choice.

Offered by Chef Patrick Edwards.

The
Charles Hooper Family
Winery and Vineyard

Visitors to the Charles Hooper Family Winery will enjoy a splendid view of the White Salmon River Valley with Mt. Hood in the distance.

Located north of Husum, Washington, the winery's special selections are White Riesling, Gewurztraminer, Chardonnay and Blush wines. Pack a picnic lunch to enjoy with a selected bottle for a delightful day's visit in Husum.

Beverlee Hooper serves the following dish, when entertaining, with rice and a large mixed-green salad. Fresh green beans also complement the lamb.

The Hoopers enjoy Gewurztraminer with Moroccan Lamb, which is equally delicious with their drier Chardonnay.

Moroccan Lamb

*This recipe is from an English friend of the Hoopers,
who had lived in Morocco.*

4 pound leg of lamb
3 medium onions, chopped
1 clove garlic, crushed
oil
salt and pepper
1/2 tsp. saffron powder or strands of saffron
1/2 cup raisins
1 heaping tsp. cinnamon
2 level Tb. honey
1 Tb. butter
1/2 cup blanched whole almonds

Pour oil 1/8-inch deep into a large heavy skillet. Add 1/3 of the
onions, garlic, 1tsp. each salt and pepper and the saffron. Heat
and stir. When really hot, put in leg of lamb, best side down.
Baste well and cover pan with a tight-fitting lid. Cook very slowly
for 20 minutes, basting occasionally. Turn lamb, cover and cook
for 30 minutes longer. Add 2 cups water and leave lamb to cook
for 1-1/2 hours until tender. While lamb stews, soak the raisins for
10 minutes in water. Pour about 3 Tb. of oil into small saucepan.
Add drained raisins, remaining onions and cinnamon. Cook for
about 30 minutes over medium heat, stirring frequently until
onions are soft and brown. Stir in the honey.

Heat butter in pan. Add almonds and brown while stirring. Drain.
Set aside.

When lamb is cooked, remove to an oven-proof platter along with
most of its juices and brown for 15 minutes at 375°. Sprinkle with
almonds and serve.

Recipe offered by Beverlee Hooper.

entrée

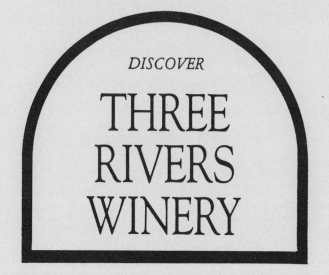

DISCOVER

THREE RIVERS WINERY

In the heart of the Columbia Gorge, three rivers converge. The White Salmon from the north, and the Hood River from the south, empty their cool, glacial waters into the mighty Columbia. They inspire the wines produced by Bill and Ann Swain. The wines from Three Rivers Winery *are created from select Columbia Gorge vineyards.*

You are invited to visit the winery, deli and tasting room located in a charming, turn-of-the-century home at 275 Country Club Road, Hood River. Easy access and return off I-84, exit #62, invites wine-lovers to stop for a taste. Wines and gift items are available for purchase.

Fillet of Sole Florentine

serves 4

4 Tb. flour
4 Tb. butter
2 cups half-and-half
3/4 tsp. salt
dash pepper
1/2 tsp. curry powder
1 10 ounce package frozen chopped
    spinach*
2 pounds fillet of sole
1/2 cup Three Rivers Gewurztraminer
1/4 cup water
Parmesan cheese

e
n
t
r
é
e

Make a cream sauce by blending flour with butter in sauce pan over medium heat. Add half-and-half and stir constantly until thick and smooth. Season with salt, pepper, and curry powder to taste. Set aside. This can be made ahead of time and reheated when ready to use.

Cook spinach in a small amount of water. Drain, pressing out excess water. Poach the sole for about 5 minutes in Three Rivers Gewurztraminer and water in a covered pan.

Butter individual casseroles or one large shallow casserole. Place spinach on bottom and lightly salt. Lift fish carefully and place on top of spinach. Add some sauce that fish has been cooked in to the cream sauce and reheat. Sauce should be medium-thick. Pour sauce over fish. Sprinkle Parmesan cheese over top and bake at 300° for about 20 minutes until bubbly. Put under broiler to brown lightly. *Voilà. Delicious!*

Serve with Three Rivers Gewurztraminer.

* Cooked broccoli tastes great as a substitute for the cooked spinach.

Recipe compliments of Ann Swain and Three Rivers Winery, Hood River.

98

Stuffed Sole

serves 4

8 sole fillets

e
n
t
r
é
e

1 cup cooked rice
1/2 cup grated Mozzarella
1/4 cup freshly grated Parmesan cheese
1/4 cup shrimp or crab meat
1/2 tsp. lemon pepper
1 Tb. butter
3/4 cup dry white wine

Wash fish and pat dry. Mix together rice, Mozzarella, half of the Parmesan, shrimp or crab and lemon pepper. Divide filling equally on fillets. Put the filling in the center of the fillets and wrap the ends up and fasten with a toothpick.

Heat butter in a skillet. Place rolls, toothpick down in butter. Add wine and reduce heat. Cover and cook for 6 or 7 minutes. Sprinkle remaining Parmesan cheese on top of each roll. Cook briefly until cheese melts.

Serve immediately.

Phillis Temple, Bend

Shrimp and Scallops with Truffle and Basil Sauce

serves 4

1 pound raw prawns, under 15 size, peeled and
  deveined
3/4 pound fresh Oregon scallops
1/3 tsp. fresh basil leaves, finely chopped
2 tsp. butter
1/2 ounce truffle*, julienne cut

2 cups heavy cream
8 small cherry tomatoes, quartered
4 Tb. olive oil
2 ounces sherry
salt and pepper

In a small heavy sauce pan, melt butter on high heat and
sauté truffles for 30 seconds. Add basil and sprinkle with salt
and pepper. Add cream and simmer over medium heat until
mixture thickens, about 10 to 15 minutes. Cool. This part of
the sauce should be done the day before if possible so the
flavors will blend.

Season prawns and scallops and flour only the prawns very
lightly. Saute the prawns in olive oil until browned. Add the
scallops and tomatoes and cook a little longer. Deglaze pan
with sherry. Add truffle sauce, return to simmer and serve
immediately over pasta or rice.

*This sauce can be made with other types of mushrooms but
  the truffle flavor is unique.

*Recipe offered by the Columbia Gorge Hotel, compliments
of Chef David Graignic.*

Salmon Soufflé with Shrimp Sauce

e
n
t
r
é
e

3 Tb. butter
3 Tb. flour
1 cup evaporated milk
1/2 cup cold water
1/4 tsp. salt
4 eggs, separated
1 pound can salmon or fresh salmon, cooked and
     flaked
lemon juice
1/2 lemon, thinly sliced

1/2 pound salad shrimp*
dillweed*

In a small saucepan, melt butter and stir in flour and salt. Cook until bubbly. Slowly add milk and water, stirring constantly. Simmer until sauce thickens*. Cool slightly.

Separate eggs, setting aside yolks, and whip whites until stiff peaks form. Pour cream sauce over egg yolks. Stir in salmon. Fold egg whites into salmon/cream mixture. Add lemon juice to taste.

Pour entire mixture into buttered soufflé or glass baking dish. Set in pan with 1 inch of hot water and bake at 350° for 35 to 40 minutes. Garnish with sliced lemon and serve hot.

* To serve with a shrimp sauce, double the cream sauce and reserve half. Add fresh shrimp to reserved sauce and season with dillweed. Spoon sauce over each individual serving.

Lee Hollomon, Silverton

Fresh Columbia River Salmon or Steelhead Teriyaki Barbecue

Teriyaki Marinade:
1/2 cup soy sauce
1/2 cup dry sherry
1/3 cup sugar
1/2 tsp. grated ginger root

*1 5 to 10 pound fresh Columbia River Salmon or
    Steelhead cut into 1-inch steaks. **

Mix marinade ingredients together in a small bowl and then warm the mixture just enough to dissolve the sugar, either in the microwave or in a sauce pan.

Pour marinade into a shallow glass baking pan and place the steaks in the marinade. Let sit 1 hour in the refrigerator, then turn the steaks over and marinate 1 hour more.

Barbecue on moderate grill for about 5 to 7 minutes on a side. Test for doneness by flaking with a fork; it should flake all the way to the bone when done.

This recipe is also excellent used with steaks that have been frozen. Thaw the steaks and proceed as above.

*The steaks near the tail are very good for children's portions as they have few bones.

Cindy usually serves this along with Rice with Garden Fresh Spinach and Onions, page 143.

Cindy Janney, White Salmon

102

Bouillabaisse

serves 6 to 8

e
n
t
r
é
e

1-1/2 cups sliced onions
1/4 cup olive oil
2 cloves garlic, crushed
3-1/2 cups stewed tomatoes
1 26 ounce can chopped clams and juice
1 quart water
1/2 tsp. thyme
1 bay leaf
1 Tb. chopped parsley
1 3-inch orange rind strip
1 tsp. salt
1/2 tsp. pepper
1 pound white fish, cut in cubes
3/4 pound fresh shrimp
1 crab, cut up
10 to 12 steamer clams
1/2 cup white wine

Sauté onions and garlic in oil until soft. Add tomatoes,
chopped clams, clam juice, water, thyme, bay leaf, parsley,
orange rind, salt and pepper. Simmer 30 minutes and add fish
and shellfish. Cook until fish is firm and clams open. Add
white wine just before serving.

*This is a special Christmas Eve dinner with the Robert Lynch
family!*

Joan Lynch, Hood River

Cioppino

1/4 cup olive oil
1 Tb. chopped garlic
1 onion, chopped
1/4 cup Sauternes
6 bay leaves
1 Tb. oregano
1 quart crushed whole peeled tomatoes, canned
2 Tb. sugar
salt and freshly ground black pepper
1 large crab
8 butter clams
8 prawns
1/2 pound bay shrimp
1/4 pound crab meat

Heat oil in saucepan. Add garlic and sauté until it is tender.
Add onion, wine, bay leaves and oregano. Cook 10 minutes
over low heat. Add tomatoes and sugar. Season to taste with
salt and pepper. Simmer 20 minutes, adding more wine if
desired. Add crab, clams, prawns, shrimp and crab meat.
Cook until clams open, about 10 to 15 minutes.

Serve with sourdough French bread.

*Compliments of Kathy's father-in-law and great chef,
    Bug Eastman.*

Louisiana Shrimp

serves 5 to 6

e
n
t
r
é
e

1/2 cup sliced onion
2 Tb. butter
1-1/2 cups cooked rice
1/2 pound cocktail shrimp, diced
1 cup light cream
1 Tb. Worcestershire sauce
2 Tb. catsup
1/4 tsp. salt
1/8 tsp. pepper
2 Tb. melted butter
1/2 cup dry bread crumbs

Sauté onion in butter until tender. Add all ingredients, except bread crumbs and 2 Tb. butter. Pour into individual baking dishes or casserole. Top with buttered crumbs.

Bake at 350° for 20 to 30 minutes. Serve hot!

Jean Tollerud, Odell

Fried Rice

serves 6

2 to 3 cups rice*
6 slices bacon, cut in 1/2-inch pieces
4 green onions, chopped
2 eggs, beaten
1 cup frozen peas and carrots
2 Tb. soy sauce, plus additional for seasoning

entrée

Cook rice and refrigerate for 6 hours or overnight.

In a large skillet sauté bacon until crisp. Add green onions and cook briefly. Stir in cold rice until combined well and hot through. Add peas and carrots, mixing well. Add eggs, stirring until they are cooked and combined with rice mixture. Sprinkle soy sauce over all, adding additional to taste.

*Leonard prefers to cook the rice in a pressure cooker or rice steamer, as the rice is best if similar to the traditional Japanese "sticky" rice.

Leonard Aubert, Mt. Hood

106

Sweet and Sour Boneless Pork

e
n
t
r
é
e

2 pounds boneless pork, cut and trimmed
1/2 cup flour
salt and pepper
1 egg
vegetable oil
1/2 cup water
3/4 cup sugar
1/2 cup white vinegar
3 Tb. catsup
3 Tb. soy sauce
1 small can pineapple chunks
1 green pepper, cut in chunks
2 Tb. cornstarch, optional

In a bowl, sprinkle pork with seasoned flour. Break an egg over pork and toss well. Heat oil in a heavy pan and brown pork. Cover and simmer until tender.

In separate pan, boil water, sugar, vinegar, ketchup, and soy sauce. Add meat, pineapple and green pepper. Cover and lower heat and cook an additional 20 minutes, stirring occasionally. The sauce may be thickened with cornstarch and water if desired.

Bev Armitage, Lumsden, Canada

The Armitage Family dearly loved the memorable year they spent here in the Hood River Valley, on a teacher-exchange program from Canada.

Barbecued Pork or Char Siu

2 pounds boneless pork

Marinade:
1/4 tsp. Five-spice
1/4 tsp. salt
2 tsp. green onion, finely chopped
1/4 cup honey
dash sugar
1 Tb. freshly grated ginger
2-1/2 Tb. dry wine
1/4 cup soy sauce
1 clove garlic, crushed

Cut pork into long thick strips. Prepare marinade by combining ingredients. Marinate pork 1 hour.

Bake for 1 hour at 375°. Baste frequently with sauce. Slice in thin slices once it has cooled slightly.

Azusa Suzuki, Parkdale

Yaya's

INTERNATIONAL CAFE

Yaya's is a Greek Restaurant, family-owned and operated by Tom and Susan Vovou, located at 207 Oak Street in Hood River. They have an extensive menu including Greek specialties, Heros, soups and salads. The dessert list boasts 12 choices of sinfully delicious Greek pastries, cheese cakes and pies.

Yaya's is committed to offering "fresh, pure, and natural" foods and their cooking methods and flavors reflect such care.

They are called Yaya's-Grandma's- in a salute to the Greek women of that generation who taught their cuisine. From the Vovou's and Yaya's--Yasoo-- to your health.

109

Spanakopita

This is a delicious spinach-cheese pie!

1 medium onion, finely chopped
1/4 cup olive oil
1 package frozen chopped spinach*

1/2 pound Feta cheese, crumbled into small pieces
6 ounces ricotta cheese
3 eggs, beaten
1/4 cup breadcrumbs

1 package phyllo pastry sheets**
1/2 cup butter, melted

Sautéonion in olive oil for 5 minutes. Add drained spinach and simmer over low heat to evaporate moisture.

In a separate bowl, mix Feta cheese with ricotta, add beaten eggs and mix well. Mix bread crumbs into spinach-onion mixture and add to cheese mixture. Stir until well blended.

Brush a 10x14-inch pan with melted butter. Unroll phyllo pastry and cut sheets in half. Brush each sheet with melted butter and place in pan to cover bottom. Use half the sheets, then fill with spinach-cheese mixture. Add remaining sheets, brushed with butter to cover top.

Bake at 350° for 40 minutes or until golden. Allow to cool 5 minutes before slicing into squares.

*   May substitute 1 pound fresh spinach, cooked and finely chopped.

**   You can find this in the frozen-foods section at most supermarkets. Allow to thaw in the refrigerator for 1 day, prior to use. This will allow the phyllo sheets to separate, for easy handling.

Recipe offered by Yaya's International Café.

Sherwood Onion Pie

serves 4 to 6

1 cup crushed crackers
6 Tb. butter

3 large onion, thinly sliced
2 eggs
3/4 cup milk
dash pepper
1/2 - 3/4 cup grated cheese, Cheddar or
Muenster

e
n
t
r
é
e

To prepare crust, crush crackers finely. Melt 4 Tb. butter in a 9 - inch pie pan, add cracker crumbs and press evenly into pan. Bake for 5 minutes at 350°. Allow to cool.

In the meantime, melt the remaining 2 Tb. butter in a large heavy skillet, add the onions and cook over low heat for 25 to 30 minutes. Stir occasionally. It is important to let them cook the full amount of time to bring out the sweetness. Spread evenly onto crust.

Beat together eggs, milk and pepper until combined. Pour evenly over onion mixture and sprinkle with grated cheese. Bake at 350° for 30 minutes, or until a knife inserted in center comes out clean.

Great as a sidedish or for a potluck!

Claire Haser, Mt. Hood

Sherwood Campground is located on Hwy. 35, 11 miles south of the community of Mt. Hood. Overnite camping, fishing, and picnic grounds are available. While visiting the campground, follow the trail up to Tamanawas Falls, a perfect addition to your day.

Spinach Cheese Pie

serves 4 to 6

1 double pastry crust (page 292), or puff pastry
12 ounces frozen chopped spinach
16 ounces ricotta cheese
2 cups diced Cheddar cheese*
1/3 cup Parmesan cheese
1 egg
1/2 tsp. salt
1/4 tsp. pepper
1/8 tsp. nutmeg
1 tsp. oregano
beaten egg for glaze

Defrost spinach, drain and squeeze dry. Mix together the spinach, ricotta, Cheddar cheese, Parmesan, egg, salt, pepper, nutmeg, and oregano.

Line an 8-inch pie plate with pastry and fill with spinach mixture. Top with the other crust. Make a few slashes in the top crust. Brush with beaten egg.

Bake at 375° for 40 minutes. Serve warm.

*You may substitute one of the cups of Cheddar with Monterey Jack cheese.

Use this same filling for croissants, page 185. This also is the same filling for phyllo triangles, page 6.

Kids even love this!

The Real Italian Pizza Pie
serves 6

pastry for a double crust (page 292)
5 eggs
1 pound ricotta cheese
2 Tb. chopped onion
1 cup Parmesan cheese
1 Tb. chopped parsley
salt and pepper
2 Tb. olive oil
1/4 tsp. marjoram
1/2 tsp. oregano
2 cloves garlic
l0 ounces tomato purée
4 ounces tomato paste
2/3 cup sliced olives
1/2 pound Mozzarella cheese
1 large bell pepper

Line a 10-inch pie dish with pastry, and roll out a top crust.

Beat the eggs, stir in the ricotta cheese, onion, parsley, Parmesan, and season liberally with salt and pepper. Set aside.

Heat the olive oil in a small saucepan. Crush the cloves of garlic into it and add the herbs. When the garlic is clear and begins to turn gold, stir in the tomato purée, tomato paste, olives and season with salt and pepper. Slice the Mozzarella thinly and slice the green pepper into matchstick-size pieces.

To assemble: Spread half of the ricotta mixture on the pastry in the pie plate. Arrange over it half the Mozzarella slices. Cover with half the tomato sauce and top with half the green pepper. Repeat all the layers and cover with the top crust. Pinch the edges together and flute the crust. With a very sharp knife, make 3 long, parallel slashes through the top crust.

Bake at 425° for 35 to 40 minutes. Let stand for 1/2 hour before serving.

Italian Sauce

1-1/2 pounds extra lean ground beef, (optional)
1 24 ounce can whole tomatoes
1 16 ounce can tomato purée
1   8 ounce can tomato paste
2 Tb. olive oil
4 cloves garlic, sliced thin
1 Tb. oregano
1 Tb. parsley
1/4 tsp. anise seed
1 tsp. basil
1 tsp. salt
1 tsp. sugar
pinch of cayenne pepper
freshly ground black pepper

Brown meat in olive oil. Add all ingredients on top of meat and simmer at least 2 hours.

If no meat is used, cover bottom of pan with olive oil. Add ingredients and simmer 2 hours.

Wonderful sauce to use for a variety of dishes: Spaghetti, pizza, lasagne, calzone.

Basic Yeast Pizza Dough

1 package active dry yeast
1 tsp. sugar
7/8 cup warm water (105° to 115°)
2-1/4 cup unbleached flour
1 tsp. salt
1 Tb. oil
cornmeal

e
n
t
r
é
e

Stir the yeast and sugar into the water in a small bowl and let rest until it proofs, about 10 minutes.

Insert the metal blade in food processor, and place the flour and salt in the work bowl. Turn on the machine and pour the yeast mixture through the tube. Process until a ball of dough forms. Add the oil and continue to process the dough for about 40 seconds.

Transfer the dough to a large oiled bowl and turn to coat. Cover and let rise until double, about 1 hour.

When ready to use, punch down and let rest for 10 minutes. Roll out, stretching with hands if necessary. Lay on a pizza pan that has been dusted with corn meal.

Cover with your choice of ingredients and bake for 15 to 20 minutes at 400°, or refer to the *Sun-Dried Tomato Pizza* recipe that follows.

Sun-Dried Tomato Pizza

serves 4

Basic Yeast Pizza Dough, previous page
1 cup Italian Sauce, page114
3 cups shredded Mozzarella cheese
1 heaping cup smokey flavored cheese*
1/2 cup garlic Monterey Jack cheese (optional)
thinly sliced pepperoni**
3 sun-dried tomatoes, minced*
8 large mushrooms, thinly sliced

Spread Italian sauce on top of crust. Combine your choice of cheeses and spread evenly over sauce, add mushrooms and pepperoni. Sprinkle on tomatoes.

Bake in a 400° oven for about 20 minutes or until cheese is bubbly. Remove from oven and let stand for 5 minutes before slicing.

* Available at the Wine Sellers, Wy'East Naturals, or deli sections
   of most supermarkets.

**May substitute meat of your choice or eliminate meat entirely for
   a vegetarian pizza.

e
n
t
r
é
e

116

Garden Stroganoff

serves 4

e
n
t
r
é
e

3 cups fresh broccoli, separated into florets
4 medium carrots, sliced
1/2 cup butter
1 pound fresh mushrooms, sliced
1 clove garlic, minced or pressed
3 Tb. flour
2 cups milk
2 Tb. soy sauce
1 tsp. chicken bouillon
1/2 cup dry white wine or apple cider
1/2 cup sliced ripe olives
1 cup sour cream
1 cup ricotta cheese
1/2 cup grated Parmesan cheese

Steam broccoli and carrots together for 5 minutes; drain. Melt butter in a large skillet and add mushrooms and garlic. Sauté until tender. In the same pan, add flour and blend until smooth. Slowly add milk, soy sauce, chicken bouillon and wine. When sauce thickens, add olives, sour cream, ricotta and Parmesan. Stir to blend. Spoon over cooked vegetables.

A meal in itself, or served on rice or pasta along with a tossed salad and a slice of Bran Muffin Bread, page 229.

Robin Laurance, Parkdale

Vegetable Indonesian

serves 3 to 4

1/4 cup oil
1/2 cup chopped onion
2 Tb. chopped green onion
3 cups cubed fresh tomatoes
3/4 cup green pepper, cut in strips
1/2 cup sliced almonds
1/4 tsp. basil
1/4 tsp. thyme
1 Tb. cornstarch or arrowroot, optional
1/2 cup sliced mushrooms, optional

Heat oil in skillet or wok over medium heat. Add both kinds of onions. Sauté, stirring frequently, until tender. Add tomatoes, green pepper, mushrooms, basil and thyme. Cook for a few minutes. Mix cornstarch with a small amount of water or broth and add to vegetables. Heat 2 or 3 more minutes stirring constantly.

Sprinkle on almonds. Serve over steaming brown or white rice.

Mexican

Flautas de Pollo

serves 6 as a main dish, or

24 as appetizers

e
n
t
r
é
e

24 6-inch corn tortillas
3 Tb. butter
1/4 cup flour
1 tsp. salt
1 cup chicken broth
1 Tb. chopped parsley
1 Tb. lemon juice
1 tsp. grated onion
dash paprika
dash ground nutmeg
dash pepper
1-1/2 cups finely diced cooked chicken
oil for frying

* guacamole (see page 121)

Heat tortillas in microwave 2 at a time for 25 seconds on high power, or wrap all in foil and heat in oven for 20 minutes at 350° to soften. (If you use the microwave method, heat 2 and then roll 2, heat & roll, etc.).

In saucepan melt butter; blend in flour and salt. Add chicken broth. Cook and stir until mixture thickens. Add parsley, lemon juice, onion and spices. Stir in chicken; cool slightly. Place about 1 Tb. mixture on each tortilla and roll tightly, securing with a toothpick. Fry in 1- inch of hot oil for 1 to 2 minutes, turning , until crisp and brown. Drain on paper towel and keep warm in a low oven while frying remaining tortillas. Remove toothpick and serve warm with guacamole as dip.

This authentic Mexican dish is wonderful as a main course, served with rice and refried beans and topped with a spoonful of guacamole, or together with an enchilada. It is equally at home as an appetizer.

Mexican Boss Salsa

6 to 8 medium, ripe tomatoes, chopped
2 large onions, finely chopped
6 to12 jalepeño peppers, seeded and finely diced
1 large bunch cilantro, washed and chopped
2 cloves garlic, pressed
salt to taste
2 Tb. lime juice, fresh or bottled

e
n
t
r
é
e

Combine all ingredients. The number of peppers used depends on your ability to handle heat! This salsa can be used on any Mexican dish as well as on tortilla chips.

Refrigerate and keep for about 1 week.

If you love hot, spicy flavor, you'll never serve any other salsa.

Hot Chile Salsa

1 28 ounce can whole tomatoes with juice
1 large onion, quartered
5 jalepeño peppers, halved, and seeded
1/2 cup packed fresh cilantro leaves
1 Tb. lime juice
1 Tb. chile powder
salt to taste

Combine all ingredients in a food processor or blender and process for about 30 seconds or to desired consistency. Increase or decrease jalepeño peppers according to taste.

RIO GRANDE
for authentic & naturally delicious Mexican Food!

Newly opened with rave revues in 1987, Rio Grande Mexican Restaurante is operated by Kate Ferguson. Resident Chef Jose Louis Solorio prepares superb, authentic cuisine for your pleasure.

Create your own selection from the many menu choices, while sipping a cold Mexican beer or Margarita. Stop in at 2nd and Cascade, downtown Hood River, for an imaginary trip south of the Border!

Guacamole con Cilantro

In the United States, this avocado mixture is usually served as a dip, but in Mexico and at Rio Grande Restaurante, it is used as a refreshing topping for many entreés.

The essential ingredients are ripe avocados with lime or lemon juice which prevents the avocados from turning off-color. How many chilies you use depends on how hot you want your guacamole. Instead of chilies, you can use a dash of chili powder.

If your guacamole isn't going to be eaten within an hour, put the avocado pit in the mixture and cover the bowl.

Cut and scoop out 2 large avocados. Add 1 chopped tomato, 1/2 small, chopped onion, 1 to 3 chopped chilies, 1 Tb. lime or lemon juice, 1 Tb. minced, fresh cilantro, and 3/4 tsp. seasoning salt.

Mash and blend all ingredients. For a smoother mixture, combine in a blender.

121

Recipe compliments of Kate Ferguson, Rio Grande.

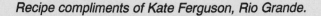

Chalupa

2 cups dried pinto beans
3 pounds boneless lean pork
1 large onion, chopped
3 cloves garlic, minced
2 Tb. chili powder
2 Tb. cumin
1 tsp. oregano
8 ounces diced green chiles
salt

tortilla chips
shredded lettuce
chopped green onions
grated cheese
chopped tomatoes
sliced olives
guacamole, page 121
salsa, page 120
sour cream
parmesan dressing, page 57, optional

Soak beans overnight. Cut meat into 2-inch chunks. Brown pork in large kettle over medium high heat. Add onion and garlic and cook until onion is limp. Add 6 cups water, chili powder, cumin, oregano and green chiles. Drain beans and add to kettle.

Cover and simmer for 2 to 3 hours, or until beans are tender. Remove meat and let cool. Shred meat at this time and return to beans. Add salt to taste. Beans may be mashed a bit if desired. Heat to serve.

Place a generous amount of chips on each plate. Spoon 1 cup pinto bean mixture on top. Top with cheese and remaining condiments.

Layered Enchiladas Laredo

1 15 ounce can tomato sauce
1 4 ounce can chopped green chiles
3/4 tsp. salt
1/2 tsp. oregano
1/8 tsp. cumin
1/2 tsp. chili powder
1/2 cup chopped green onion
1 cup grated Cheddar cheese
1 cup grated Monterey Jack cheese
12 corn tortillas
vegetable oil

Combine tomato sauce, chiles and seasonings. Cover and simmer about 10 minutes. Combine cheeses and onion; reserving 1/2 cup.

Heat oil in small frying pan and dip each tortilla in to soften. Place tortilla in baking dish. Top with 2 Tb. sauce and 1/4 cup cheese mixture. Repeat layers, ending with tortillas. Pour remaining sauce over stack. Bake at 350° for 25 minutes. Top with remaining cheese and continue baking until cheese melts. Cut into wedges and serve.

entrée

Creamy Chicken Enchiladas

2 whole chicken breasts
1 small can chopped green chiles
1 8 ounce package cream cheese
1 Tb. butter
1 small onion, finely chopped
1/2 pint heavy cream
1 dozen flour tortillas
1/2 pound Monterey Jack cheese, shredded
1 small can sliced black olives

* options-sour cream, guacamole, salsa
shredded cabbage

Bake chicken breasts in foil at 350° for 25 minutes. Chop
into small pieces. Sauté onion in a Tb. of butter until limp.
Add chicken, cream cheese and chiles to onion. Put about
3 Tb. of chicken mixture on a tortilla and roll up tight. If
tortillas are not soft enough to roll nicely, microwave 2 at a
time on high power for 30 seconds, or heat all in foil in low
oven for 15 minutes to soften.

Line filled tortillas in a 9x13- inch baking dish and pour
cream over to cover. Cover with shredded cheese and top
with black olives. Bake for 30 minutes at 325° or until
cheese is bubbly.

To serve, top with sour cream, guacamole and salsa if
desired. These may also be served on a bed of shredded
cabbage or lettuce.

e
n
t
r
é
e

Chicken Tortilla Bake

6 whole chicken breasts
1 dozen corn tortillas
1 can cream of mushroon soup
1 can cream of chicken soup
1 cup of milk
1 onion, grated
1 7 ounce can green chile salsa,
   (or any mild salsa)
1 pound grated Cheddar, or 1/2 Monterey Jack,
   1/2 Cheddar

Bake chicken in foil in a 350° oven for 40 minutes. Remove from oven and save juice. Cool and cut into medium size pieces. Cut tortillas into 1-inch pieces. Make a sauce out of the soups, milk, onion and salsa. In large buttered baking dish, place 3 Tb. of the chicken broth. Add half of the tortillas, then a layer of chicken, then a layer of sauce. Repeat with layers of tortillas, layer of chicken and end with a layer of sauce. Sprinkle the grated cheese over the top.

Refrigerate overnight. This is important to allow flavors to blend. Bake at 300° for 1 to 1-1/2 hours.

Virginia Wheeler, Hood River

entrée

125

Fajitas

Fajitas have many different versions. The one basic ingredient is either chicken or beef. This is a simple version you can easily prepare in your own kitchen.

e
n
t
r
é
e

1 to 1-1/2 pounds sirloin steak or
    boneless, skinless chicken breasts, thinly
    sliced on the diagonal
1 white onion, thickly sliced
one green bell pepper, thinly sliced

flour tortillas
sour cream
cilantro
guacamole (see page 121)
salsa (see page 122)

Marinade:
1/2 cup olive oil
1/2 cup lime juice, fresh or bottled
3 cloves crushed garlic
salt and pepper

Before you begin, heat at least 15 or more tortillas in foil in a 300° oven for 10 minutes. Keep warm.

Combine all ingredients for marinade and mix well. Marinate meat of your choice for at least 2 hours. Heat a large skillet over medium high heat until very hot. Remove meat from marinade and add to skillet. Place cut onions and pepper in marinade while you cook the meat. Stir-fry until almost done, about 5 minutes for either beef or chicken. Remove the meat and set aside, keeping warm. Add the vegetables to the pan and stir-fry until tender, about 5 minutes. Use the marinade while cooking both meat and vegetables to keep from sticking. You should use most of the marinade by the time you are done. Return chicken to the pan and combine with vegetables.

Serve in the pan in which you cooked. Have at the table: the warm tortillas, chicken/vegetable mixture, sour cream, chopped cilantro, guacamole and salsa. People create their own Fajita by placing a small amount of the mixture in the center of the tortilla, topped with the works, or on the side. Roll and enjoy!

The perfect tortillas for Fajitas are Juanita's "Gorditas" flour tortillas.

126

Cinco de Mayo Tamales

serves 6 to 8

corn husks, soaked

Dough:
2/3 cup margarine
2 cups Masa Harina
1 tsp. garlic salt
2 tsp. chile powder
1/4 tsp. baking powder
1-1/3 cups chicken broth

8 ounces pepper jack cheese, cut into 24 cubes

1-1/2 cups green chile salsa

Cover corn husks with warm water and let soak for 2 hours or overnight.

Prepare dough by first whipping the margarine until fluffy. Mix together the masa, garlic salt, chile powder and baking powder. Blend in the masa mixture and broth into the margarine and mix until the dough holds together well. Cover with a damp cloth and keep cool until ready to use.

For each tamale, select a wide, pliable, soaked corn husk. Lay it out flat with the tip pointing up, and place 2 Tb. of masa dough in center. Push a cube of cheese into masa. With your fingers, spread masa up and around cheese. Fold sides of husk over masa, then lift ends up over filling. With a thin strip of husk, tie tamale to hold shut. Repeat with other husks.

Place tamales, tied ind up, arranging them loosely enough so steam can circulate freely, in a steamer on a rack over at least 1-inch of boiling water. Cover and boil gently for 45 minutes. Serve or keep warm in steamer for up to an hour. If made ahead, let cool, then cover and refrigerate until next day; reheat by steaming as directed for 20 minutes.

To serve, open husks and spoon salsa over tamales.

entrée

127

Vegetable Burritos

serves 4 to 6

2 Tb. oil
2 cloves garlic, minced
1 large onion, sliced
1/2 pound mushrooms, sliced
1 large green pepper, cut in thin strips
2 carrots, sliced
2 zucchini, sliced
2 tomatoes, cut in wedges
1 7 ounce can diced green chiles
1/2 cup sliced olives
1 tsp. chili powder
1 tsp. salt
1/2 tsp. cumin
1/2 tsp. oregano
1 cup Monterey Jack cheese, shredded
1 cup Cheddar cheese, shredded
1 dozen flour tortillas
guacamole, see page 121
sour cream
toasted sunflower seeds

Sauté garlic and onion in oil over medium-high heat. Add mushrooms, green pepper, carrots, zucchini, tomato, chiles, olives, spices and herbs. Bring to a boil, lower heat, cover and simmer until vegetables are barely tender, about I0 minutes.

Uncover and gently boil, stirring occasionally, until all the liquid has evaporated and vegetables are tender. When they are done, stir half of each kind of cheese into vegetables. Turn into a shallow ovenproof dish and sprinkle with remaining cheese.

Serve with warm tortillas*. Spoon vegetables down center of tortilla, top with a bit of guacamole, sour cream and sunflower seeds.

* To heat tortillas, wrap 10 to12 in foil and bake at 350° for 15 to 20 minutes.

Swiss Chard Enchiladas

serves 4

1 dozen corn tortillas
1 cup grated Cheddar or Monterey Jack cheese
1 medium onion, finely chopped
1-1/2 pounds Swiss chard
1/2 tsp. salt
3 Tb. vegetable oil
2 cloves garlic, minced
3/4 cup sour cream
1 can green chile enchilada sauce or
*   any commercial sauce of your choice*
oil for frying

Wash the chard, making sure to clean out all sand. In a large saucepan put about 2 inches of water and bring to boil. Add the chard and salt and let it boil for about 5 minutes. Drain and chop. The chard should be crisp tender. In the same pan heat the oil and garlic. Add the chard and cook for a few minutes.

Heat the oil and fry the tortillas quickly, one- by-one. Drain on paper towels and keep warm. * Put some of the filling across each tortilla with a spoonful of sour cream , then roll up and place in dish. Pour the enchilada sauce over and sprinkle with the grated cheese. Bake in a 325° oven until warm through, about 25 minutes. Sprinkle with onion and serve.

* You may use the microwave method and eliminate frying each tortilla. Place two at-a-time in the microwave for 30 seconds on high, fill and roll as you go.

Casserole Chiles Rellenos

3 7 ounce cans whole green chiles
1 pound Monterey Jack cheese, grated
1 pound Cheddar cheese, grated
3 eggs, beaten
3 Tb. flour
1 small can evaporated milk
1 15 ounce can tomato sauce

e
n
t
r
é
e

Wash chiles, remove any seeds and pat dry. In a 9x13-inch baking pan, layer half of the chiles, then half the cheeses. Repeat the layers, reserving 1/2 cup cheese for a topping.

Beat the eggs, add the flour and milk and beat until blended.

Pour the egg mixture over the chiles and cheese. The casserole can be refrigerated at this point, if desired.

Bake at 350° for 30 minutes. Spread tomato sauce evenly over the top, sprinkle with the reserved cheese and bake 15 minutes longer.

Cut into squares to serve.

Mexican Rice

3 cups rice, uncooked
3 cups sour cream
1/2 cup melted butter
1/2 cup diced green chiles
1/2 cup chopped hot green chiles
1 small jar diced pimentos
3/4 pound Monterey Jack cheese, grated
3/4 pound Cheddar cheese, grated

Cook rice according to package instructions. Mix sour cream, butter, chiles, and pimentos into cooked rice. Place half of the mixture into a buttered 2-quart casserole dish. Top with the Monterey Jack cheese. Add the remaining half of rice mixture and top with the Cheddar cheese.

Bake at 350° for 25 to 30 minutes, until heated through and the cheese melts.

compliments of Leona Rosentreter, Anchorage, Alaska

Pasta

Gorge-ous Seafood Lasagne

serves 8

1 pound bay scallops
*1 pound fresh Oregon shrimp ***
1/3 to 1/2 cup butter
3/4 cup chopped green onions
1 clove garlic, crushed
1/4 tsp. thyme
1/3 cup flour
1 cup chicken broth
1 cup heavy cream
1/2 cup dry white wine
8 ounces lasagne noodles
3/4 pound shredded Swiss cheese

e
n
t
r
é
e

Rinse seafood well. Chop scallops into 1/2-inch pieces if using larger variety. Melt 2 Tb. of butter in a frying pan. Add onion, garlic and thyme. Cook until limp; about 2 minutes. Add seafood and cook for 3 minutes. Remove from heat and drain, reserving broth. Drain until cool.

Melt 3 Tb. butter in same frying pan and add flour, blending until it turns light golden brown. Remove from heat and slowly add broth, cream and wine. Return to heat and bring to a boil stirring constantly until mixture thickens.

Cook lasagne noodles according to package directions. Drain and rinse with cold water to stop further cooking.

Pour the juice from the scallops and shrimp into a small pan. Cook over medium heat until it is reduced to 3 tablespoons. Add to cream mixture.

Butter a 9x13- inch pan and lay 1/3 of the lasagne noodles in it. Cover the noodles with 1/3 of the sauce, then 1/3 of the seafood, then 1/3 of the cheese. Repeat layers.

Bake at 350° for 20 minutes covered with foil. Remove foil and continue to bake for an additional 20 minutes. Let stand for about 15 to 20 minutes before cutting.

* May use only scallops or a combination of seafoods equalling 2 pounds.

132

Pasta with Salmon and Cream Sauce

e
n
t
r
é
e

2 cups heavy cream
4 Tb. butter, divided
1 tsp. salt
freshly grated nutmeg
1 pound fresh, thin pasta
1 Tb.Parmesan cheese
2 cups cooked salmon
1-1/2 Tb. dillweed
parsley

Simmer the cream and 2 Tb. butter in a small saucepan. Add salt and nutmeg and continue to simmer until cream is reduced by one-third. Add Parmesan cheese, salmon and dill and remove from heat.

Cook pasta according to directions on package. Drain pasta and toss with remaining 2 Tb. butter. Add cream sauce. Garnish with parsley. Easy and delicious!

Linguine with Clams

serves 4

2 7 ounce cans chopped clams in juice
1/3 cup extra virgin olive oil
3 large cloves garlic, minced
salt
freshly ground black pepper to taste
3 Tb. fresh parsley, chopped
1 pound fresh or dried pasta, any long thin variety
1/2 cup heavy cream

Put the olive oil in a frying pan and add the garlic. Brown well but do not burn. Add the clam juice, salt and pepper and cream. Add the parsley and clams. Heat but do not boil.

Meanwhile cook the pasta according to package instructions. Drain well. Then pour the hot clam sauce over it. Mix the pasta well with the sauce and serve immediately.

Lost Lake Lasagne

serves 6

2 whole boneless, skinless chicken breasts
1 medium onion, finely chopped
8 ounces fresh mushrooms, sliced
1/4 cup butter
2/3 cup dry white wine
1/2 tsp. dried tarragon
1/2 tsp. salt
1/2 tsp. pepper
8 lasagne noodles, cooked and drained
1 8 ounce package cream cheese
1/2 cup half-and-half or cream
1/2 cup sour cream
1-1/2 cups grated Swiss cheese
1 cup Mozzarella
1/2 cup toasted sliced almonds

Cut chicken into 1-inch pieces. Sauté the onions and mushrooms in butter until tender. Add chicken, wine, tarragon, salt and pepper. Reduce heat, cover and simmer for 6 to 8 minutes or until chicken is tender.

Meanwhile, halve lasagne noodles lengthwise. Curl each noodle into a ring about 2 to 3 inches in diameter and place in a 9x13-inch baking dish. Using a slotted spoon, spoon chicken/mushroom mixture into the center of each ring.

Add cream cheese, cream, sour cream and half of each of the 2 cheeses to the liquid remaining in pan. Stir until smooth and then pour over lasagne. Top with remaining cheese and sprinkle with almonds. Bake, covered, at 325° for 35 minutes.

Lost Lake is the best known of the many lakes found in Hood River County. Mt. Hood as its back-drop makes a perfect mirror image on a calm day. Spend a day or days enjoying boating, camping, fishing, hiking or swimming. A 3 mile trail around the lake is a perfect afternoon hike.

Baked Italian Lasagne

serves 12

1 pound Italian sausage or ground beef
1 clove garlic
1 Tb. parsley flakes
1 Tb. basil
1-1/2 tsp. salt
1 large can tomatoes
2 6 ounce cans tomato paste
10 ounce package lasagne noodles
3 cups small curd cottage cheese or ricotta
2 beaten eggs
2 tsp. salt
1/2 tsp. pepper
2 Tb. parsley
1/2 cup freshly grated Parmesan cheese
1 pound Mozzarella cheese, thinly sliced

Brown meat and add next 6 ingredients. Simmer covered at least 2 hours. Cook noodles in boiling salted water until tender. Drain.

Meanwhile combine cottage cheese or ricotta with eggs, seasonings and Parmesan cheese.

Spoon a little sauce into the bottom of a 9x13-inch baking pan. Layer half of the cooked noodles. Spread half the cottage cheese mixture over noodles, half the Mozzarella cheese, and half the meat sauce. Repeat layers.

Bake at 350° for 45 minutes. Let stand 10 to 15 minutes to set before cutting in squares.

Doris Suriano, White Salmon

Nic's Vegetarian Pasta

serves 6

1 pound penne or rigatoni noodles
1-1/2 cups cottage cheese
1/2 cup sour cream or plain yogurt
4 Tb. butter
2 zucchini, sliced
1/8 pound mushrooms, cut in half
1 pound firm tofu, cut in 1/2-inch cubes
1 bunch chopped green onions or
    1 small onion, chopped
crushed garlic to taste
1 cup grated cheese (Monterey Jack, Romano,
    Provolone, or Cheddar)
2 tsp. dried parsley
1 tsp. dried basil
2 tsp. soy sauce or to taste
salt

Cook pasta according to instructions on package. When finished, toss with butter and mix in cottage cheese and sour cream. Meanwhile, sauté zucchini, onion, garlic and mushrooms in 1 Tb. butter for 5 minutes. Add soy sauce and herbs. Add this to the noodle mixture. In same skillet melt 1 Tb. butter and sauté tofu for about 5 minutes or until golden. Sprinkle with soy sauce. Add tofu to the noodles. Stir in the grated cheese and transfer to a buttered casserole dish and bake at 350° for 30 to 40 minutes.

This pasta dish is Nic's favorite!

Garden Pasta Primavera

serves 6 to 8

1 pound linguine, fresh or dried
1 pound broccoli, broken in florets
2 small zucchini, sliced
1/2 pound asparagus, cut in 1-inch pieces
1/4 cup olive oil
2 whole cloves garlic, peeled
1/2 pound mushrooms, cut in half
1/4 cup fresh basil or 1 tsp. dried
1/2 cup frozen baby peas
1 pint cherry tomatoes
1/4 cup chopped parsley
1 tsp. salt
pepper to taste
1/4 tsp. crushed red pepper flakes
1/4 cup butter
3/4 cup heavy cream
2/3 cup freshly grated Parmesan cheese

Cook pasta according to package directions, while preparing
the following ingredients. Steam broccoli, zucchini, and
asparagus until vegetables are crisp-tender, about 7 minutes.
Drain and place in large bowl.

Meanwhile heat olive oil in large skillet or wok. Add garlic and
mushrooms. Cook for 3 minutes. Add peas, tomatoes, basil,
parsley, salt, pepper, and pepper flakes. Continue to cook
2 minutes longer. Add this mixture to the vegetables in bowl.

Melt butter and stir in cream and cheese. Cook until cheese is
melted and sauce is smooth. Add cooked linguine and toss
together. Add to vegetables, toss and serve.

This pasta dish is extremely impressive in taste and color. A
beautiful spring meal to serve guests with a tossed green
salad, bread, and a bottle of fine Northwest white wine.

This recipe comes from the kitchen of Doris Suriano, a most
marvelous "Swedish-Italian" cook.

e
n
t
r
é
e

137

Pepper Noodle Stir Fry

serves 4 to 6

1 package cayenne pepper noodles*
   (available at some markets and at delis)
2 whole chicken breasts, boned and skinned, cut
   in bite-size pieces**
4 Tb. butter
2 carrots, peeled and sliced diagonally
1/4 pound mushrooms, cut in half
1 medium zucchini sliced in rounds
1 bunch green onions cut in 1/2-inch lengths
2 stalks celery sliced diagonally
1 clove garlic, minced or pressed
salt to taste
pinch of cayenne
sour cream
1 or 2 large avocados
cilantro

In a large skillet melt 2 Tb. of the butter and add garlic and chicken. Stir fry for about 5 minutes until chicken is almost done. Remove chicken from pan and set aside. Add the remaining butter and stir fry the vegetables until crisp and tender, about 5 minutes. Return chicken to the pan and stir, combining vegetables and chicken. Season.

Meanwhile cook the noodles according to package directions. If using the variety indicated, cook about 3 minutes. Drain.

Place adequate amount of noodles on each plate and top with vegetables and chicken. Add a spoonful of sour cream on top with a sprig of cilantro. Garnish with sliced avocado.

* If these noodles are not available , you may use plain fettuccine.

** This entire dish may be made without the chicken as a vegetarian entrée.

Avocado Twist

8 ounces spiral egg noodles
1/4 cup butter
1 clove minced garlic
1 large avocado
lemon juice
5 slices bacon, diced and cooked crisp
chopped fresh parsley
freshly grated Parmesan cheese

e
n
t
r
é
e

Cook the noodles according to package instructions. Meanwhile, melt butter and stir in garlic. Drain noodles when done and toss with garlic butter. Dice avocado into bite-size pieces and sprinkle with lemon juice. Fold avocado and bacon into noodles. Turn onto serving platter and garnish with parsley. Pass grated cheese separately.

Delicious and fast!

Wy'East Florentine

1/2 cup butter
1   10 ounce package frozen chopped spinach, thawed and drained
12 ounces bacon, fried and crumbled
1 pound fettuccine, cooked and drained
1 egg, slighly beaten

1-1/2 cups heavy cream
1-1/2 cups grated fresh Parmesan cheese
1 tsp. salt

Melt butter in a large skillet. Add the spinach and bacon and heat through.

Add the cooked noodles and toss. Stir together the cream and egg and add to the noodles. Add the cheese. Salt to taste. Toss to mix well. Cover and heat through for a few minutes. Serve immediately.

HOOD RIVER
HOTEL
RESTAURANT & BAR

Warm European Charm in the
Heart of the Columbia Gorge

The Hood River Hotel, recently restored to its 1913 splendor, offers its guests turn-of-the-century charm without sacrificing modern conveniences. It was recently recommended by "Best Places to Stay in the Pacific Northwest".

The rooms are decorated with antiques reminiscent of the hotel's origins; many offer spectacular views of the Columbia River. You don't have to be a hotel guest to enjoy breakfast, lunch or dinner. In season, the sidewalk café is a fine place to take your espresso and watch the activity on Oak Street.

Pasquale's Alfredo Sauce

Sauté in olive oil: minced garlic, chopped bacon, mushrooms, diced red and green bell peppers. Add salt and pepper to taste. Add whipping cream and a pinch of nutmeg. Let simmer slowly, stirring occasionally and allow sauce to reduce to desired consistency. To change the flavor, you may want to add grated parmesan cheese or sour cream. Serve over fresh fettuccine.

Pasquale notes that classic Alfredo sauce is only reduced whole cream. Anything else you may want to put in is up to you. Enjoy!

Offered by Hood River Hotel

140

Pasta Deluxe

serves 4

e
n
t
r
é
e

8 to 12 ounces pasta (macaroni or seashell)
2 cups small curd cottage cheese
1 cup sour cream
garlic salt
pepper
1 egg, beaten
1/8 tsp. dry mustard
1 to 1-1/2 cups grated Cheddar cheese
1/4 cup Parmesan cheese
paprika

Cook pasta in salted boiling water until tender. Drain.

Combine cottage cheese, sour cream, egg, seasonings and dry mustard. Stir in 1 cup Cheddar cheese and pasta.

Spoon into greased 3-quart casserole dish. Top with remaining 1/2 cup Cheddar and Parmesan cheeses.

Bake at 350° for 40 to 45 minutes, until bubbly and set. Do not over cook.

Christie Smith, Parkdale

Pacific Crest Pasta

serves 4

3 medium zucchini, sliced
1 onion, sliced and separated into rings
1/4 cup cooking oil
3 tomatoes, peeled and chopped
1-1/2 tsp. crushed dried basil
1-1/2 tsp. dillweed
1/2 tsp salt
8 ounces dried pasta (corkscrew, penne,etc.)
1 Tb. flour
1 cup sour cream
1/2 cup crumbled Feta cheese

e
n
t
r
é
e

In a large pan cook zucchini and onion in oil until tender, about 5 minutes. Add tomatoes, basil , dillweed and salt. Cover and simmer for 10 minutes.

While this mixture is simmering, cook pasta according to package directions. When done, drain and keep warm.

Stir flour into sour cream. Stir 1 cup of tomato mixture into sour cream . Return all to saucepan. Heat but do not boil. Transfer warm pasta to serving dish and spoon on tomato mixture. Sprinkle crumbled Feta cheese on top.

─────────────────────

In Oregon, the National Scenic Pacific Crest Trail starts in the north at the Bridge of the Gods in Cascade Locks, travels west near Lolo Pass and around the slopes of Mt. Hood, south past Mt. Jefferson and the Three Sisters, and continues along the Cascade Mountains to Crater Lake and south near Mt. Ashland. It has proven to be extremely popular with hikers and horseback riders who have visited all or parts of the trail.

On the Side

Rice with Garden Fresh
Spinach and Onions

1 medium Walla Walla Sweet onion, minced
2 Tb. olive oil
1 pound fresh spinach, washed and chopped
1 Tb. white vinegar
1 tsp. dried dill weed
4 cups cooked rice*
1/2 cup Parmesan cheese
salt and pepper to taste

Sauté the onion in 2 Tb. olive oil in a wok over medium high heat until the onion is transparent. Add the spinach and sauté until it cooks down, less than 5 minutes. Add the vinegar and dill weed and cook until most of the moisture in the spinach has evaporated.

Reduce heat to low and add the cooked rice and toss and stir until well mixed and heated. Add the Parmesan cheese and toss. Add salt and pepper as desired.

Serve immediately while hot!

* White rice is best. Add 1 Tb. bran while cooking for more fiber!

Cindy serves this with Teriyaki Barbecued Salmon, page 102.

Cindy Janney, White Salmon

Wild Rice Casserole

serves 4 to 6

2/3 cup wild rice
2 cups beef consommé
1/4 cup butter
1/4 cup onion, diced
1/2 cup celery, diced
1/2 cup mushrooms, sliced
2 Tb. toasted, slivered almonds

Wash and drain rice. Simmer rice and consommé, covered, for 40 minutes, or until tender. Sauté onion, celery and mushrooms in butter until tender. Drain rice and add sautéed vegetables. Sprinkle with almonds.

A perfect dish alongside a thick slice of Prime Rib or with Garlic Baked Chicken, page 80.

Vegetable Rice Pilaf

serves 6

2 cups long grain rice
3-1/2 cups boiling water
1-1/2 tsp. salt

1/2 tsp. curry powder
1/2 tsp. salt
1/8 tsp. black pepper
1/2 cup chicken bouillon broth

3/4 cup melted butter
1/2 cup sliced green onions
1 small green pepper, diced into 1/2-inch pieces
1 small sweet red pepper, diced into 1/2-inch
*   pieces*
2 stalks celery, sliced
1/2 cup sliced water chestnuts
1/2 cup sliced almonds, toasted

Wash rice with cold water. In a heavy saucepan combine
rice, water and salt. Cook covered, over low heat for 20
minutes, or until tender. Fluff up rice with a fork. Add the
chicken bouillon and seasonings.

Sauté the vegetables in butter for 5 minutes. Fold into hot
rice. Sprinkle with almonds.

Offered by Sister Margaret Boehm, F.S.E., Bridal Veil
Franciscan Villa.

on the side

145

Zucchini-Chile Bake

2 cups cooked brown rice
3 medium zucchini, thinly sliced
1 7 ounce can chopped green chiles
2 cups grated Monterey Jack cheese
1 large tomato, thinly sliced
salt and pepper
2 cups sour cream
1 tsp. oregano
1 tsp. garlic salt
1/4 cup chopped green pepper
1/4 cup chopped green onion
2 Tb. chopped fresh parsley

Steam zucchini for 5 minutes. Set aside. Place cooked rice in
a buttered 3-quart casserole dish. Top with chopped chiles.
Sprinkle with half of the cheese.

Arrange zucchini slices over cheese. Add tomato slices and
season with salt and pepper.

Combine sour cream, oregano, garlic salt, green pepper and
green onion. Spoon over tomato layer. Sprinkle with cheese.

Bake at 350° for 45 to 50 minutes. Top with parsley.

Shredded Zucchini Bake

1-1/4 to 1-1/2 pounds zucchini
4 eggs
1/4 cup flour
3/4 cup grated Parmesan cheese
1-1/4 tsp. salt
1/4 tsp. pepper
1/4 cup chopped parsley
1/4 cup thinly sliced green onion
1 clove garlic, minced
1 tsp. oregano
2 tomatoes, sliced
bacon crumbs

Shred zucchini. Press out moisture. Set aside.
In a mixing bowl, beat eggs adding flour and half the cheese,
salt, pepper, parsley, onion, garlic and oregano. Mix well to
blend.

Stir in the zucchini and turn into a greased 1-1/2 quart shallow
baking dish.

Arrange sliced tomatoes on top. Press lightly into zucchini
mixture. Add bacon if desired. Sprinkle with remaining
cheese over top.

Bake uncovered at 350° for 30 minutes or until set in the
center.

Helen Claire Smith, Hood River

Artichoke Casserole

serves 4 to 6

2 packages frozen artichoke hearts
2 Tb. butter
2 Tb. flour
8 ounces cream cheese
2/3 cup milk
1/3 cup water
1 can ripe olives, sliced
8 to 10 green onions and tops, chopped
2/3 cup grated Parmesan cheese

Thaw artichokes and arrange in a shallow 1-1/2 quart casserole dish.

In saucepan, melt butter, blend in flour. Cook until golden brown.

Remove from heat, blend in cream cheese. Add milk and water gradually. Bring to a boil, stirring constantly. Remove from heat, add olives and onions.

Cover artichokes with sauce and sprinkle Parmesan on top. Bake at 325° for 1-1/2 to 2 hours.

Christie Smith, Parkdale

on the side

Spinach Cheese Bake

serves 4

1 10 ounce package frozen chopped spinach
2 Tb. flour
2 eggs, beaten
4 ounces cream cheese, cubed
3/4 cup Mozzarella cheese or Cheddar
*   cheese, cubed*
1/4 cup butter, cubed
1-1/2 tsp. Instant minced onion
1/2 tsp. salt
1/4 cup butter, melted
1/2 cup fine bread crumbs
1/3 cup Romano cheese

Cook spinach covered in the microwave on high power for 6 minutes, stirring after 3 minutes. Drain.

Stir in flour, blend in eggs, cheeses, cubed butter, onion and salt. Cook again in microwave, covered, for 8 to10 minutes, stirring 2 times. Set aside.

Combine melted butter and bread crumbs. Sprinkle over spinach and top with Romano cheese. Brown under broiler for a few minutes. Serve immediately.

Becky Schmuck, Husum

Snow Pea Mushroom Sauté

serves 4

4 *medium carrots, sliced on the diagonal,*
  1/2 inch thick
4 *Tb. butter*
1 *clove garlic, minced*
1/2 *cup morel mushrooms, or 1 cup button*
  mushrooms, cut in half
1/2 *pound snow peas, strings removed*
3 *tsp. rice wine vinegar, or raspberry vinegar*
salt and pepper

Blanch carrots in boiling water until crisp-tender, about
4 minutes. Drain and rinse in cold water.

Melt butter in a heavy skillet over medium heat. Add garlic
and stir for about 2 minutes. Do not burn. Add carrots and
cook 2 minutes. Add mushrooms and snow peas and cook
for 2 minutes. Add vinegar and stir until snow peas are crisp-
tender. Season with salt and pepper.

Wah-Gwin-Gwin Sauté

serves 4

1-1/2 Tb. olive oil
1/2 pound yellow summer squash, cut in 1/2-inch
   pieces
1/2 pound zucchini, cut in 1/2-inch pieces
1 small onion, chopped
1/4 pound tomatoes, peeled, seeded and
   chopped
1/2 tsp. dried marjoram, crumbled or use fresh if
   available

In a large skillet, on medium-high, heat oil until hot. Add the summer squash, zucchini, and onion. Season with salt and pepper to taste. Sauté, stirring for 2 minutes. Add the tomatoes and marjoram. Steam covered for about 3 minutes, just until vegetables are tender. Do not overcook.

View Wah-Gwin-Gwin Falls, as the sparkling waters cascade and tumble from the Columbia Gorge Hotel's "backyard" to the Columbia River 206-feet below. The falls have been a romantic spot for generations of Northwesterners and a thrilling sight for thousands of visitors from around the world.

on the side

Vegetable Medley

2 small onions, sliced
1 medium head cauliflower, cut in florets
1 bunch broccoli, cut in florets

4 Tb. butter
4 Tb. flour
1 cup milk
8 ounces cream cheese

1/2 pound mushrooms, cut in half

2 cups bread crumbs
2 Tb. butter
1/2 tsp. garlic powder

2 cups grated Cheddar cheese

Steam onions, cauliflower and broccoli until tender, about 7 minutes. Drain.

While vegetables are cooking, make a white sauce; melt butter in a small saucepan, add flour and stir while cooking until mixture is well blended and bubbly. Add milk slowly and cook until smooth. Add cream cheese, stir until melted. Add salt and pepper to taste.

Combine mushrooms with steamed vegetables and place in a buttered baking dish. Pour sauce over all.

Melt 2 Tb. butter in a small frying pan and add garlic powder and bread crumbs. Cook briefly until brown and flavors are combined. Spread over top of vegetables and top with grated cheese.

Bake at 350° for 25 minutes.

Twin Peak Stuffed Potatoes

4 large russet potatoes
2 Tb. butter
1/4 to 1/3 cup milk
1/2 cup Cheddar cheese
3 ounces cream cheese
2 Tb. minced green onion
1/4 tsp. nutmeg
1/4 tsp. salt
pepper and paprika

Bake potatoes at 425° until done. Cool slightly and then cut in half lengthwise. Scoop out potato leaving 1/4-inch of potato in shells. Whip potato, milk, cheeses, onion and seasonings until smooth and fluffy. Mound mixture into shells. Refrigerate* until ready to bake. Bake at 400° for 20 minutes.

* Potatoes may be frozen up to 1 month. Bake frozen potatoes at 375° for 35 minutes.

Costello Potatoes

6 large potatoes, peeled, and thinly sliced
3 Tb. olive oil
1 green pepper, sliced
1/2 large onion, sliced
2 cups shredded Cheddar cheese
1 bunch green onion, including tops, finely
*   chopped*
salt and pepper

Pat potatoes dry with paper towel. Do not immerse in water. Heat olive oil in large skillet. Add potatoes, green pepper and onion. Fry until crisp and brown, turning with a spatula. Turn out onto a serving platter and top with cheese. Cover with a lid or foil to allow cheese to melt. Remove lid and sprinkle with green onions.

Ann Costello

153

Heather's Heavenly Potatoes

Heather loves these delicious potatoes. This is her favorite thing to prepare when it is her turn to cook.

4 large russet potatoes
1 bunch fresh broccoli, or 1 package frozen
1-1/2 cups grated Cheddar cheese
4 Tb. butter, softened
1 to 2 tsp. Dijon mustard

Wash potatoes, and prick with a fork. Bake at 400° for 1 hour or until done.

While potatoes are baking, prepare broccoli. If using fresh, cut into small pieces and steam for 5 minutes on stove top or microwave in a covered dish for 3 minutes in 1/4-inch water. If using frozen, thaw. Broccoli should be crisp-tender.

Remove potatoes from oven and slit open tops. Fluff with a fork.

Combine butter and amount of mustard desired. Divide evenly between potatoes. Top with broccoli and sprinkle with cheese. Return to oven for 10 minutes, until cheese melts.

For variety, add bacon, onion, sour cream, any type of cheese, ground beef, etc. Use your imagination!

Heather Laurance, Parkdale

Milly's Mexican Corn

2 cups fresh corn, cut from the cob
1 small can diced green chiles
3 Tb. minced onion
1 clove garlic, minced
2 eggs, beaten
1 8 ounce can tomato sauce
1/2 tsp. chili powder
1/2 tsp. cumin
salt and pepper to taste

1 to 2 fresh tomatoes
2 cups grated cheese, half Cheddar, half
  Monterey Jack

Mix together the first 9 ingredients. Pour into a lightly
buttered 9-inch square baking dish.

Cut tomato in half and lightly squeeze out juice. Slice
tomatoes and arrange on top of corn mixture. Sprinkle with
cheeses. Bake at 350° for 30 to 40 minutes.

*Created very cleverly from Milly's garden surplus for a larger
than expected group of friends.*

Helen Claire Smith, Hood River, a special friend to many

Soups

Old Theater Mercantile Antiques and PieBirds Café share space in the Historic Valley Theater building located in Parkdale at the foothills of majestic Mt. Hood. The restored 1937 vintage movie theater is on the National Register of Historic places.

Enjoy excellent French-style cuisine during lunchtime or dinner which offers an espresso bar and freshly baked goods, while sitting among fine antiques and memorabilia.

Greek Lemon Soup

8 cups chicken broth
1 cup long grain rice
1/4 tsp. white pepper
3 egg yolks
1/4 cup fresh lemon juice
1/2 cup whipping cream
3 Tbs. chopped fresh parsley

Whisk egg yolks and lemon juice together.

Bring chicken broth and pepper to full boil. Add rice, simmer and cover. Cook 20 minutes or until rice is tender. Remove from heat. Ladle 1 cup of soup into yolk mixture, whisking thoroughly and add back to remaining soup. Heat to scald and whisk in the cream and parsley. Do not let boil.

Garnish with a slice of fresh lemon and parsley.

Recipe offered by Chef Maurice Lemon, PieBirds Café.

Carrot Soup

serves 4

1 small onion, chopped
1 Tb. butter

1 cup shredded carrots
1-1/4 cups peeled, sliced potatoes
salt and pepper
pinch sugar
3 cups chicken stock
1 Tb. chopped parsley
1/2 Tb. chopped chervil

Sauté onion in butter until tender. Add carrots and potatoes. Add salt, pepper and sugar. Cook uncovered for 5 minutes. Add chicken stock. Cover and simmer for an additional 15 minutes.

Purée, reheat and add parsley and chervil. Serve with bread and salad.

Great after a long day on the ski slopes.

Phyllis Temple, Bend

Chinese Hot and Sour Soup

2 ounces dried Shiitake mushrooms*
2 cups hot water
2 cups thinly sliced mushrooms
1 pound tofu
3 Tb.corn oil
3 cups slivered Chinese cabbage
1-1/2 Tb. soy sauce
2 Tb. red wine vinegar
1 tsp. pepper
1 tsp. chili-pepper oil*
3 cups water
2 cloves crushed garlic
2 Tb. cornstarch
3 Tb. cold water
1 Tb. sesame oil*
2 eggs, well beaten
4 green onions, thinly sliced

Soak theShiitake mushrooms in the first 2 cups hot water until soft (about 20 minutes). Drain and reserve the liquid. Cut away the hard stem and slice thinly.

Thinly slice the tofu and then cut into slivers.

Heat a wok or soup pot on high heat. Swirl in the oil and heat. Stir in both types of mushrooms and toss for 2 minutes. Stir in the cabbage, soy sauce, vinegar, pepper and pepper oil. Add the reserved mushroom liquid, the additional 3 cups water, garlic, and tofu. Bring to a boil and simmer for 3 minutes.

Mix the cornstarch with the 3 Tb. water and sesame oil. Add to the soup and simmer until thickened.

Drizzle in the beaten eggs while stirring. Stir in the green onions. Serve and enjoy the warmth!

*Available in the Oriental section of most supermarkets.

s
o
u
p

Hood River Village Resort

The Hood River Village Resort welcomes you to visit the panoramic Columbia River Gorge.

Complementing your stay, executive chef Bart Livengood offers a spectacular 65 item Sunday brunch, and on Sunday evening, a mouth-watering prime rib dinner. For your convenience, the lower floor provides an international coffee shop and daily full-service dining. The dinner menu includes both formal and casual selections, with special fare for deck-goers.

At the Hood River Village Resort your business and pleasure are easily combined. Uniquely designed with a 180° view of the Columbia River, your visit to the resort will ensure a memorable experience.

Louisiana Creole Soup

2 cups catsup
3 cups water
2 cups tomato sauce*
2 medium green peppers, julienne cut
1 medium onion, julienne cut
2 ounces diced red pepper
2 ounces diced green chilies
2 stalks celery, diced
4 tsp. Cajun seasoning (meat, poultry or seafood)
green onion, diced

Combine ingredients in a large pot and heat slowly. Simmer one hour. Garnish with diced green onion.

*Home-canned tomatoes may be substituted for the tomato products. If catsup is not used, add 1 ounce sugar.

Recipe offered by Bart Livengood, and Hood River Village Resort.

Hood River Village Resort

MULTNOMAH FALLS

Multnomah Falls is easily accessible from both
I-84 and the narrow Columbia River Scenic
Highway.

This spectacular 620-foot free-falling waterfall is
the second highest in the western United States.
In the winter months, the falls turn into a
masterpiece of sculptured ice. . .a breathtaking
sight! Other months hikers can follow a trail to
the top and watch the stream plummet into its
deep pools.

At the base of the falls, you can watch for Coho
Salmon in the stream and visit the historic
Multnomah Falls Lodge. This impressive stone
lodge was constructed in 1925. Today it serves
as a full-service restaurant and gift shop. It is
open daily year-round and invites the public to
fine dining. You may choose either the dining
room, enclosed patio, coffee shop, or the
outdoor snack bar.

The Multnomah Falls Visitors Center has
information on the early settlement days along
the river, and provides a history of the geologic
events that shaped the great Columbia.

Other nearby falls to see while traveling along the
Columbia River Scenic Highway are Horsetail,
Shepperds Dell, Oneonta Gorge, Wahkeena and
Bridal Veil.

Boston Style Clam Chowder

1-1/2 cup diced onion
1-1/2 cup diced celery
1/2 cup diced green pepper
1/2 cup diced bacon or 3 Tb. oil
2 cups chopped clams
4 cups clam nectar
1 quart half-and-half, heated
2 Tb. clam base (optional)
3 bay leaves
salt and white pepper to taste
4 cups pre-cooked diced potatoes (with cooking
*   liquid)*

Sauté onion, celery and green pepper with bacon or in oil.
Add clams and nectar. Simmer until vegetables are tender.
Add heated half-and-half, clam base, bay leaves, salt and
white pepper. Thicken with roux* to desired consistency.
Add potatoes with liquid. Simmer 10 minutes (do not boil).
Garnish each serving with a pat of butter.

Compliments of the Multnomah Falls Lodge

* Roux: heat 1/2 c. butter or oil; add 1 c. flour, stirring
constantly to form a heavy paste. Cook on low heat 15 to 20
minutes, stirring often to prevent burning. May be stored in
refrigerator until needed.

Bob's Clam Chowder

1/2 pound bacon
1 large onion, chopped
4 cans chopped or minced clams, including juice
1 can each, cream of potato, cream of celery and
     cream of onion soups
2 medium potatoes, diced
milk

s
o
u
p

Cut bacon in small pieces and brown until crisp. Add
chopped onion and sauté. Add clams, soups and potatoes.
Pour in enough milk until the chowder is the consistency
desired. Bring to a slow boil, reduce heat and simmer for 20
minutes, stirring often.

Bob Gosslee, Mosier

163

Scallop Chowder

1/4 cup butter
1-1/2 cups diced onion
1 tsp. parsley
1/2 tsp. dill weed
1/2 cup flour
5 cups clam juice
2 Tb. white wine
1 bay leaf
1 cup half-and-half
1/2 pound scallops

s
o
u
p

Melt butter in a heavy pan. Sauté onions in butter until limp. Add parsley and dill and cook for 2 minutes. Blend in flour until it makes a smooth paste and cook for 2 more minutes. Set aside.

IInto a separate stock pot add clam juice, white wine and bay leaf. Bring mixture to a boil. Add a roux* to boiling stock and whisk until smooth. Bring to a boil over medium heat, stirring occasionally. Reduce heat to low and add scallops and half-and-half. Simmer for 10 minutes. Garnish with parsley and a patof butter if desired.

*Roux: heat 1/2 c. butter or oil; add 1 c. flour, stirring constantly to form a heavy paste. Cook on low heat 15 to 20 minutes, stirring often to prevent burning. May be stored in refrigerator until needed.

Vegetable Cheese Chowder

1/2 cup butter
1 large onion, finely chopped
1 cup finely chopped celery
1 cup finely chopped carrot
1 zucchini, finely chopped
2/3 cup flour
6 cups chicken stock
1 cup heavy cream
1/2 pound grated Cheddar cheese
salt and pepper to taste

Melt butter in a large saucepan. Add vegetables and sauté until tender. Add flour and cook, stirring constantly until well blended. Slowly add chicken stock. Stir until smooth. Cool slightly.

Transfer to food processor or blender and purée (do this in batches).

Return to pan and add cream and cheese. Stir until the cheese has melted. Season and serve. Garnish with parsley if desired.

Cascade Corn Chowder

serves 4 to 6

5 slices bacon
1 medium onion, thinly sliced and separated
   into rings
2 medium potatoes, peeled and diced
1/2 cup water
1   17 ounce can cream-style corn
2 cups milk
1 tsp. salt
dash pepper
butter

In a large saucepan, cook bacon until crisp. Remove bacon, crumble and set aside. Reserve 3 Tb. bacon grease in pan. Add onion slices and cook until light brown. Add diced potatoes and water. Cook over medium heat until potatoes are tender (10 to15 minutes). Add corn, milk, salt and pepper. Heat through. Pour into bowls and garnish with reserved bacon and a pat of butter.

Ellen Larsen, Hood River

s
o
u
p

166

Fiery Potato Soup

serves 6

8 slices bacon
5 fresh jalapeño peppers, seeded and finely chopped
1 medium onion, chopped
2 stalks celery, sliced
1/2 cup diced red bell pepper
4 cloves garlic, minced
2 pounds new potatoes, peeled and diced
1 pint heavy cream
1/4 cup dry white wine
3 cups milk
salt and pepper to taste
cilantro for garnish

Cut bacon in 1/4-inch slices. Fry until crisp; drain and set aside. Discard all but 2 Tb. of the drippings.

Add onion, celery, both peppers and garlic to the pan drippings. Cook until all vegetables are soft.

Meanwhile, place the cubed potatoes in a pot and cover with 1-1/2 cups water. Boil until tender, about 15 minutes.

Stir in the vegetables, cream, milk, wine, salt and pepper. Heat but do not boil. Garnish with bacon and cilantro.

Creamy Mushroom
and Potato Soup

1/2 cup sliced onion
1/2 cup mushrooms, sliced
2 Tb. butter
4 medium potatoes, diced
1-1/2 tsp. salt
1 cup water
1/4 cup flour
1-1/2 tsp. paprika
pinch of cayenne pepper
1 cup sour cream
2-1/2 cups milk
cooked, crumbled bacon   (optional)

s
o
u
p

Cook onion and mushroom in butter. Add potatoes, salt and 1 cup water. Cover and cook 10 minutes until potatoes are tender. Mix flour, paprika, cayenne, and sour cream into a paste and add to potatoes. Stir in milk. Heat to just before boiling, cook for 1 minute. Serve. Garnish with bacon if desired.

A wonderfully hearty soup for a cold winter evening.

Wendy Anderson, Lumsden, Canada

JoAnn's Mushroom Soup

serves 6

1/2 to 3/4 pound mushrooms, thinly sliced
1 Tb. butter
1 tsp. paprika
1 Tb. flour
2 Tb. finely chopped parsley
4 cups beef stock
1 egg yolk
1 cup sour cream, warmed

Sauté mushrooms in butter with paprika until golden brown.
Sprinkle mushrooms with flour and parsley. Gradually stir in
beef stock and simmer slowly for 30 minutes. Beat egg yolk
slightly; blend with sour cream and turn into a soup tureen.
Slowly pour hot soup over it, stirring well. Serve
immediately.

JoAnn von Lubken, Hood River

Cream of Morel Soup

4 Tb. butter
1 quart fresh Morel mushrooms, sliced
1 onion, thinly sliced
3 celery stalks, thinly sliced
2 cloves garlic, minced
1 cup beef or vegetable stock
3 cups whole milk
salt and pepper to taste

Melt the butter in a large saucepan. Add the Morels and cook until soft. Using a slotted spoon, remove mushrooms; set aside. Place onion, celery and garlic in remaing butter/mushroom broth, and cook until tender. Add beef or vegetable stock and milk to the saucepan. Bring just to a boil and reduce heat. Stir in the reserved, cooked Morels. Simmer without boiling for about 20 minutes. Salt and pepper to taste.

This soup is a wonderful way to use wild Morels, a seasonal favorite!

soup

Stonehedge Inn
at Wildwood Acres

It all began in 1905, when a Portland family built a beautiful summer home at Wildwood Acres. The home was owned privately until 1975, when it was turned into a restaurant and restored to original construction to maintain the atmosphere of this historic home.

It was named Stonehedge, after the unique stone hedges, built prior to World War I, which surround the classic home.

Now the tradition is being carried on by Jean Harmon. Stonehedge Inn credits Chef Mark Dower's choice of a superlative menu and mouth-watering dessert tray. Order a 4-course meal or a light supper. The perfect after theater stop for dessert and a nightcap.

Atmosphere and friendly service combined with excellent cuisine makes Stonehedge Inn the choice of many. Pacific Northwest magazine's honorable award for "Best Unknown Restaurant" in 1988 went to Stonehedge Inn at Wildwood Acres.

Black Bean Soup with Curried Sour Cream

2 pounds black beans, soaked overnight
3 quarts chicken stock
3 quarts beef stock
1 sachet with 3 bay leaves, 1 tsp. cracked black
    peppercorns, 1 tsp. whole thyme
2 pounds bacon, diced
3 cups diced yellow onions
8 cloves garlic, peeled and crushed
2 green bell peppers, diced
2 red bell peppers, diced
3 stalks celery, diced
1/2 cup tomatoes in purée
1/2 cup sherry
1/2 cup burgundy
2 Tb. curry powder
1 Tb. coriander powder
1/2 tsp. cayenne
1 tsp. cumin
2 Tb. lemon juice
1/2 pint sour cream
1/2 tsp. curry powder
3 Tb. cilantro, chopped

Drain beans. Simmer beans with sachet in chicken and beef stock until tender. Remove sachet.

Meanwhile, in a large pan, sauté bacon, remove from pan, leaving fat. Sauté onions, celery, peppers, and garlic until tender. Add sherry and burgundy, let simmer. Then add all herbs and spices, lemon juice and tomatoes in purée to beans.

Simmer, correct seasoning with salt and pepper. Combine the sour cream, curry powder and cilantro. Top each serving with a dollop of the curry /sour cream mixture.

Offered by Chef Mark Dowers, Stonehedge Inn, Hood River

Hearty Bean Soup

2 cups mixture of any of these dry beans (kidney,
  pinto,adzuki, baby lima, split pea, lentil,
  garbanzo, black bean or small white beans)
2 quarts water
2 Tb. safflower oil
2 cloves garlic, minced
2 large onions, chopped
3 stalks celery, diced
2 carrots, diced
1/2 green pepper, chopped
2 bay leaves
1/2 tsp. marjoram
1/2 tsp. basil
1/2 tsp. thyme
2 Tb. soy sauce
freshly ground pepper
salt to taste
4 Tb. parsley
1 28 ounce can whole tomatoes

Soak beans in 6 cups water overnight. Drain beans, rinse and
cook in 2 quarts water for about 3 hours or until beans are
tender.

Meanwhile, sauté in oil the garlic, onion, celery, carrots and
green pepper for about10 minutes. Add spices and continue
cooking 3 more minutes. Add to cooked beans along with
parsley and tomatoes. Simmer for one hour over low heat.
Remove bay leaves and adjust seasonings.

Even better the second day!

*Compliments of Kathy's husband, Erik, who recently has
been doing more cooking than she has!*

Spicy Black Bean Soup

serves 6

1 pound dried black beans
1/4 pound bacon, chopped
4 to 6 cloves garlic, minced
2 stalks celery, minced
1 large carrot, peeled and diced
1 medium onion, diced
2 jalapeño chili peppers, seeded and diced
1 bay leaf
1 Tb. chili powder
1 tsp. ground cumin
1/2 tsp. cayenne pepper
1/2 tsp. black pepper
8 cups chicken or vegetable stock

Soak beans overnight. Drain. Transfer to a large saucepan. Cover with cold water. Boil for 20 minutes. Drain, and set aside.

Cook bacon in heavy saucepan until brown and crisp. Mix in garlic, celery, carrot, onion, jalapeño and bay leaf. Cook until vegetables are tender, about 10 minutes. Add spices. Stir for about 1 minute to blend flavors.

Add beans and broth. Simmer until beans are tender, stirring occasionally, about 1-1/2 to 2 hours. Season with salt to taste.

Spicy Black Bean Soup will mellow in flavor if refrigerated.

Minestrone à la Milanese

1-1/2 cups dried kidney beans
3 to 4 cloves garlic
1 large onion, chopped
5 Tb. olive oil
3 large potatoes
2 carrots
5 to 6 zucchini
1-1/2 cups cut string beans
1/2 cup leeks
pinch of celery seeds
2 tsp. basil
1 tsp. oregano
pinch of marjoram
1/2 head savoy cabbage
1/2 cup cooked rice
6 to 7 tomatoes, cubed
1 cup grated Parmesan cheese
3 to 4 Tb. butter

Soak beans overnight. Simmer for 1-1/2 hours in large kettle with garlic, onion, oil and 4 quarts water.

Cut potatoes in large pieces and add to soup. Add sliced carrots, zucchini and leeks and string beans. Season with herbs and simmer 45 minutes.

Slice cabbage thinly and stir into soup along with rice.

Simmer 20 minutes more, adding water if too thick. About 5 minutes before serving, add cut tomatoes, Parmesan cheese, butter and parsley.

Marilyn Smith, Hood River

Country Style Soup

serves 6

Make a mixture of 6 to 8 different types of beans for a total of 2 cups:

pinto	kidney
black-eye	navy
split pea	adzuki
black	lima

3 quarts water
3 ham hocks
1 bay leaf
1/2 tsp. marjoram
1/2 tsp. oregano

1 28 ounce can tomatoes, undrained
2 onions, chopped
4 stalks celery, chopped
3 cloves garlic, minced
salt and pepper to taste

1 pound link sausage, cut in 1/2-inch pieces
3 boneless, skinless chicken breasts, cut in
  bite-size pieces

1/2 cup red wine
1/2 cup chopped fresh parsley

Wash and drain peas and beans. Simmer with first 5 ingredients, covered, for 2 hours. Remove skin and bones from ham hocks. Add next 4 ingredients. Salt and pepper to taste. Simmer for 1-1/2 hours. Add sausage and chicken; simmer another 30 minutes.

Before serving, stir in wine and parsley.

This is one of the heartiest soup you'll ever serve!

Compliments of Helen Vik

Hearty Hamburger Soup

1 tsp. butter
1 pound ground beef
3 medium onions, sliced
1 28 ounce can tomatoes
salt and pepper to taste
1 tsp. basil
2 bay leaves
6 cups beef stock
3 medium carrots, sliced
3 celery stalks, sliced
3 medium potatoes, sliced
1 package frozen chopped spinach
1/3 cup small sea-shell pasta
1/2 tsp. Worcestershire sauce
1/4 tsp. Tabasco sauce

Melt butter, add beef and cook slightly. Add onions, tomatoes, salt, pepper, basil, bay leaves, and beef stock. Bring to a boil; cover and simmer for 1 hour. Add remaining vegetables*except spinach and cook 1 hour longer. Stir in shell pasta and spinach during last 12 to 15 minutes of cooking time. Correct seasoning.

*May add 6 to 7 cups of shredded cabbage with vegetables.

Tortilla Lime Soup

serves 4

2 tsp. oil
1 small can chopped, green chiles
1/3 cup onion, chopped
4 cups chicken stock or broth
1-1/2 cups cooked chicken, shredded
salt to taste
1 tomato, chopped
1 Tb. lime juice, or more to taste
4 lime slices

3 corn tortillas
oil for frying

Heat oil in a large pan, add onion and cook until tender. Add chiles, broth, chicken, and salt to taste. Cover and simmer for 20 minutes. Add tomatoes and simmer 5 minutes longer. Stir in lime juice.

Meanwhile, cut tortillas in 1/2-inch strips. Fry in hot oil until brown and crisp.

Ladle soup into bowls and top with tortilla strips. Garnish with a slice of lime.

Sandwiches

Dilla

Spicy Cheese Sandwich

sourdough bread
mayonnaise
sliced tomato
Swiss cheese, sliced
Cheddar cheese, sliced
Spicy Sauce, see below
sprouts

To make sandwich: spread mayonnaise on 2 slices of bread. On one side, add tomato slices and lots of Swiss and Cheddar cheese. Spread 1 to 2 Tb. Spicy Sauce on other piece of bread. Close sandwich and place on a microwave-proof dish, cover and microwave for 1 minute, until cheese melts slightly. Garnish with sprouts.

Spicy Sauce:
1 cup catsup
1/4 cup chopped onion
2 tsp. cumin
1-1/2 Tb. chili powder
1/2 tsp. cayenne
1 Tb. lemon juice

To make sauce: combine all ingredients and simmer for 30 minutes. This sauce may be stored in the refrigerator until needed.

THE COFFEE SPOT

The Coffee Spot, owned and operated by Tony Meierbachtol, is a gourmet coffee house-delicatessen which features a variety of fresh ground coffee drinks, homemade soups, salads, entrées and delectable desserts. Locals know it as "The Spot" and continually return to choose from the array of exceptional deli sandwiches.

Enjoy a muffin, waffle or quiche in the morning hours with your coffee. An occasional Northwest musician in the evening is also a treat at The Spot.

Each afternoon, from 3 to 5, is "Java Hour" and all coffee drinks are half price.

Available for your pleasure are a variety of regional and national wines and local and imported beers.

For your catering needs, The Coffee Spot is happy to work with you on a custom designed menu for an event to remember.

Cheese and Pesto Sandwich

This cheese and pesto sandwich is one of the creative offerings that has become one of the favorites at "The Spot". The pesto will keep when refrigerated for at least a few weeks, and frozen for 4 months. Better yet, freeze your fresh basil and use it as needed to make a much fresher tasting pesto year-round. This pesto recipe is a variation of the traditional pinenut recipe which will allow making your pesto when specialty products are not available.

Pesto:
2 cloves garlic
1/4 cup walnuts or pinenuts
3/4 cup Kasseri or Parmesan cheese
1/2 cup olive oil
1/4 cup safflower oil
1-1/2 cups fresh basil leaves

In food processor, chop garlic with metal blade. Leave garlic in bowl, add walnuts and chop again. Add cheese in 1-inch chunks. Process with garlic and nuts. Mix olive and safflower oils together. Add alternately with basil leaves, pouring oil slowly into the above mixture. Purée all in processor until smooth.

For Sandwich:
Spread mayonnaise on both pieces of your favorite bread (sourdough seems to be most popular), add four slices of Provolone cheese to one side. Toast both slices of bread . Spread a thin, even layer of pesto on melted cheese. Toast 30 more seconds or until bread is golden. Add tomato slices and generous amount of crisp, fresh red leaf lettuce.

Recipe offered by Tony Meierbachtol, The Coffee Spot.

Calzone

serves 4 to 6

Crusty dough:
1 Tb. dry yeast
1 cup warm water
1/2 tsp. salt
2 tsp.olive oil
2-1/2 to 3 cups flour

s
a
n
d
w
i
c
h

Dissolve yeast in warm water for 5 minutes. Stir in salt and oil. Gradually mix in enough flour to make a soft dough. Turn dough onto a well-floured board and knead until smooth and elastic, adding more flour as needed. Place in a greased bowl, cover and let rise in a warm place until doubled, about 1 hour.

Filling:
2 to 3 Tb. olive oil
1 small onion, sliced
1 clove garlic, minced
1/2 pound mushrooms, sliced
1 small green pepper, sliced
1 small carrot, thinly sliced
1 8 ounce can tomato sauce
1 2-1/2 ounce can, drained, sliced olives
1 tsp. basil
1 tsp. oregano
1/4 tsp. crushed red pepper
2-1/2 cups shredded Mozzarella cheese
3/4 cup Parmesan cheese
salt and pepper

While dough rises, prepare filling. In a large frying pan, cook the onion and garlic over medium heat in oil. When soft add mushrooms, green pepper, and carrot. Continue cooking until vegetables are limp. Stir in tomato sauce, olives, basil, oregano and red pepper. Simmer uncovered about 5 minutes. Let cool while dough rises. When ready to assemble, stir in 2-1/2 cups shredded Mozzarella cheese and 3/4 cup Parmesan cheese. Add salt and pepper to taste.

After dough has risen, punch down and divide into 4 or 6 round balls. Roll on lightly floured board into 8- inch circles. Brush each circle lightly with oil. Spread the filling over half of each dough circle. Fold in half and press edges together, seal and crimp. Place on greased cookie sheet that has been dusted with cornmeal. Prick tops with fork and brush lightly with oil.

Bake at 450° for 15 to 20 minutes.

Serve plain or with sauce.

Sauce:
1 8 ounce can tomato sauce
1 small can sliced mushrooms
2 Tb. chopped onion
1/2 tsp. oregano
1/2 tsp. basil

Prepare sauce by combining ingredients and simmering 5 to 10 minutes.

Betty's Hot Crab Sandwiches

1 can crabmeat
1/2 cup sharp Cheddar cheese, grated
1/4 cup celery, finely chopped
2 tsp. chopped green onion
mayonnaise, about 1/4 cup
English muffins or sandwich rolls

Combine the crabmeat, cheese, celery, and green onion with enough mayonnaise to moisten. Spread on top of buttered muffins or rolls.

Bake at 400° until hot and bubbly, about l0 to l5 minutes.

Betty Rea, Corona del Mar

Grilled Cheese and Comice

1/4 cup butter, softened
1/8 tsp. each: nutmeg, cinnamon, and ginger
4 slices firm white bread
1 large ripe pear, peeled and sliced in 1/4-inch
    slices. (Comice, Bartlett or D'Anjou)
2 1/4-inch slices Gruyere cheese
2 1/4-inch slices Mozzarella or cheese of your
    choice: smoke or garlic Monterey Jack, Fontina
    or Cheddar

In a small bowl cream together the butter and spices. Spread butter on both sides of bread. Layer one slice Gruyere, 1 slice pear, 1 slice Mozzarella and another slice of pear. Cover with second slice of bread. Compact the sandwich slightly to retain shape. Heat a heavy skillet over medium heat and add sandwiches. Grill on both sides until golden. Serve warm and garnish with an additional slice of pear.

Croissant Fillings

Croissants are used for all occasions. We wanted to share some of our favorite fillings so that you may take a simple frozen croissant and change it from plain to fancy. You can purchase unbaked, plain, rolled croissants in the freezer section of most supermarkets. These fillings are helpful in creating something special for breakfast, brunch, lunch or dinner.

Remove croissants from freezer about 20 minutes before you plan to fill. Let set at room temperature until partially thawed, about 20 minutes. Unroll and lay flat. Place about 2 Tb. of most mixtures at the wide end and roll back up. Lay on cookie sheet 5 or 6 to a pan, with tip of croissant on the under side so that it will not retract when baked. Brush with an egg wash. Let rise covered until doubled in size. Usually plan on at least 4 hours, depending on the temperature of your home. You may also cover and let rise overnight in a cooler spot. Bake at 350° for 14 to 18 minutes.

Suggestions:

spinach-cheese filling, page 112
cream cheese and jelly
baby shrimp and cream cheese
crab sandwich filling, page 184
lemon curd, or lemon curd and cream cheese
chocolate chips
ham and Swiss cheese
turkey and cranberry sauce
grated Cheddar cheese
pesto and Provolone cheese
Brie

s
a
n
d
w
i
c
h

Ruth's Tuna Tacos

1 can solid white albacore tuna, water packed
3 Tb. mayonnaise
1 medium tomato, diced
2 Tb. onion, diced
1 to 3 jalapeño peppers, seeded and diced

flour tortillas

sprouts, optional*
sunflower seeds, optional*

s
a
n
d
w
i
c
h

Combine first 5 ingredients. Warm flour tortillas and place 1/4 cup tuna mixture inside tortilla. Roll tightly. Serve warm or cold.

Ruth McAlexander, Parkdale

* We thought you could add either or both of these ingredients for a different twist!

Veggie Sandwich

whole wheat bread
cream cheese, softened
avocado slices
green onions, finely chopped
green pepper, finely chopped
mushrooms, thinly sliced

finely chop together equal amounts:
celery and carrots
cabbage, red or green
Cheddar cheese, grated
tomato slices
alfalfa sprouts

Lightly toast bread. Spread with creamcheese, top with slices of avocado. Combine green onions, green pepper and mushrooms. Place 1 to 2 Tb. of this on top of avocado. Add 1 to 2 Tb. of vegetable mixture.

Sprinkle with cheese and broil until cheese melts. Garnish with tomato slices and sprouts. Serve open face.

Breakfast
&
Brunch

Dilla

Mucho Nacho Omelette

filling for 6 omelettes

The following recipe, offered by Multnomah Falls Lodge, gives you a wonderful filling for your next 3-egg omelette.

Filling:
1/2 c. extra-lean ground beef, cooked*
1 cup refried beans
1 small can chopped green chiles
1/2 cup sour cream
1-1/2 cups shredded Cheddar cheese
1 tsp. tabasco sauce
1 tsp. chili powder
1/2 tsp. cumin
1/4 tsp. black pepper
1/4 tsp. granulated garlic
salt to taste

Mix above ingredients, putting equal amounts into 6 omelettes.

Topping:
1-1/2 cups shredded Cheddar cheese
1 cup diced tomatoes
1/2 cup sliced black olives
1/4 cup sliced green onion

guacamole, page 121
salsa, page 122
chips

Put on omelette; heat in broiler 1-1/2 to 2 minutes or until heated through. Add guacamole. If filling is cold, warm up in a microwave oven. Garnish with salsa and chips.

* May substitute shredded cooked chicken, ground turkey, or eliminate the meat altogether.

Compliments of the Multnomah Falls Lodge

Spring Asparagus Eggs

serves 4

20 spears fresh asparagus or
1 10 ounce package frozen asparagus
3 Tb. butter
3 Tb. flour
1-3/4 cups milk
1/2 tsp. salt
1/8 tsp. pepper
3/4 cup shredded sharp Cheddar cheese
6 hard-boiled eggs, sliced
4 slices bread, toasted
paprika

Steam asparagus for 5 to7 minutes or until crsip-tender. If using frozen, follow package instructions. Set aside cooked asparagus. (You also may reheat leftover asparagus.)

Melt butter in a heavy saucepan over low heat; add flour and cook 1 minute, stirring constantly. Gradually add milk; cook over medium heat, stirring constantly until thick and bubbly. Add salt, pepper and cheese; stir until cheese melts. Gently fold in hard-boiled eggs.

Arrange 1/4 of asparagus spears on each slice of toast; spoon 1/4 of egg sauce on each. Sprinkle lightly with paprika.

Spring Asparagus Eggs and a fruit salad make a light and tempting combination for an early afternoon meal.

Overnight Layered Eggs

8 to 10 servings

1 can condensed cream of mushroom soup
   (undiluted)
3 Tb. dry sherry or milk
1-1/2 cups each:shredded Cheddar cheese and
   Monterey Jack cheese
18 eggs
3 Tb. milk
2 tsp. parsley flakes
1/2 tsp. dill weed
1/8 tsp. pepper
4 Tb. butter
1/4 pound mushrooms, thinly sliced
1 small bunch green onions, chopped
paprika

In a pan over medium heat or in the microwave, stir sherry
and soup together until smooth and hot. Set aside.
Combine both cheeses, toss lightly to mix; set aside. Beat
together in a large bowl: eggs, milk, parsley, dill weed and
pepper; set aside.

In a large skillet over medium heat melt butter. Add
mushrooms and onion and cook until limp, about 5 minutes.
Add egg mixture to same pan and cook, gently lifting eggs
until the are softly set. Remove from heat. Spoon half the
scrambled eggs into a 9x13-inch baking pan. Spoon half the
soup mixture over the eggs, then sprinkle with half the
cheese. Repeat layers and sprinkle with paprika.

Cool, cover and refrigerate until the next day. Bake
uncovered at 300° for 1 hour or until hot and bubbly. Let
stand for 10 minutes before cutting.

Mexican Oven Omelette

serves 6 to 8

8 eggs. beaten
1-1/4 cup milk
1 tsp. garlic
7 ounce can diced chilies
1/4 cup chopped green onion
1 tomato, chopped
8 ounces Cheddar cheese

salsa
sour cream

Beat together the eggs, milk and garlic. Combine with chilies, green onions, tomato and cheese.

Pour into a greased 1-1/2 quart shallow baking dish and bake at 350° for 40 minutes until set.

Serve with sour cream and salsa.

A family recipe handed down to Kathy from her aunt, Dorothy LaRue

El Buenos Dias Pasta

serves 6

2 Tb. cooking oil
2 cups cooked noodles - thin noodles work best
(spaghetti, linguine, fettuccini)
1 large tomato, seeded and diced
1 small onion, chopped
2 fresh jalepeño peppers, seeded and chopped
fine
salt and pepper to taste
3 eggs, beaten
1/2 cup half-and-half
3/4 cup shredded Monterey Jack or Gruyère
cheese

Heat oil in 10 to 12- inch frying pan. Add the noodles and toss until they are warm through and slightly brown.

Meanwhile combine the tomato, onion and peppers. Pour this combination over the noodles and toss together. Season.

Mix together the eggs and milk. Pour over the noodles. Let cook on medium for about 5 minutes. Sprinkle cheese on top. Cover, reduce heat and let stand for another 5 minutes. The eggs should be set.

Remove from heat and slice in pie shaped wedges. Serve immediately. You may garnish with a sprig of cilantro if desired.

This dish makes a wonderful brunch entrée or a light supper.

THE FLYING L RANCH

The Flying L Ranch *is a Country Inn and retreat facility, nestled in the Ponderosa pines and meadowland of the Glenwood Valley at the base of the 12,276-foot Mt. Adams. For over 43 years, the ranch has been owned and operated by the Lloyd family, who first opened it for guests in 1960. Bed and Breakfast guests love the beauty and solitude of the ranch surroundings, while enjoying Ilse Lloyd's scrumptious breakfasts in the rustic cookhouse.*

At least 25 guests can be accommodated in 12 rooms (including one cabin), and the variety of facilities make the Flying L highly desirable for group gatherings, workshops, seminars, family reunions, and weddings.

St. Mark's Eggs

serves 8 to 10

8 slices bread, buttered on 1 side
8 slices sharp Cheddar cheese
10 eggs
4 cups milk
1 tsp. salt
1/2 tsp. white pepper
1 tsp. dry mustard
4 slices bread

Place 8 slices of bread buttered side down in a 9x13-inch baking dish. Cover each slice of bread with a slice of cheese. Beat together the eggs, milk, salt, pepper, and mustard. Pour over the bread and cheese. Cube 4 more slices of bread and cover the other ingredients. Place in the refrigerator overnight.

Bake at 325° for about 1 hour.

Recipe offered by The Flying L Ranch, compliments of Ilse Lloyd.

Breakfast Pizza

1 package crescent refrigerator rolls
1-1/2 to 2 cups Mozzarella cheese, shredded
3 eggs
3/4 cup milk
1 Tb. dry onion or 3 green onions, chopped
8 slices bacon, cooked and crumbled
parsley flakes

Line a greased 9x13-inch baking dish with the flat crescent rolls. Pat with hands to make sure there are no air holes. Sprinkle the cheese over the dough.

Beat the eggs, milk and onion together. Pour egg mixture over cheese and dough. Sprinkle with bacon and parsley. Bake at 375° for 18 to 20 minutes.

Cheryl Madsen, Hood River

Erin's French Crepes

Erin loves to surprise her parents with these lovely crepes when it is her turn to cook!

3 eggs
1 cup milk
3 Tb. melted butter
3/4 cup flour
1/2 tsp. salt
2 Tb. sugar, optional*

Beat together eggs, milk, butter, flour, salt and sugar until smooth. Melt a bit of butter in small fry pan or crepe pan over medium heat. Pour 1/4 cup batter into the pan and immediately tilt and turn the pan so that batter will cover the surface evenly. Turn the crepe when under side is lightly browned, about 2 to 3 minutes, and cook the other side for 2 more minutes. Slide crepe out onto waxed paper to cool. Repeat with remaining batter, adding butter after each crepe as necessary.

Fill with your choice of filling and roll.

Crepe fillings:

Apples, walnuts, and raisins sautéed in butter and sprinkled with cinnamon, sugar and lemon juice.

Your favorite jam or preserves; roll and sprinkle with powdered sugar.

Fill with cottage cheese, roll and top with jam and sour cream.

* For dinner crepes, omit sugar and add Parmesan cheese. Fill with chicken, broccoli, asparagus, or mushrooms and cheese sauce.

Erin Eastman, Mt. Hood

The Grand Old House

This Victorian mansion was built in 1860 by Mary and Erastus Joslyn, the area's first white settlers. It is filled with history and an unequalled romantic ambiance.

This Bed and Breakfast has seven lovely guest rooms that offer charm and comfort. The main floor has a large living room, a cozy lounge and three dining rooms specializing nightly in fresh seafood, steaks, and chicken dishes as well as vegetarian cuisine. The dining room is open to the public Tuesday through Sunday evenings. Breakfasts are delightful and hearty.

The acre of grounds features a hot tub surrounded by a Japanese garden and an English rose garden.

Hosts Greg and Cyndy DeBruler welcome you to *The Grand Old House*, located in Bingen just 1 mile east of the Hood River Bridge, on Hwy. 14. Interesting tales of history can be told of the house and its past occupants. The DeBrulers will be happy to share their knowledge of the area, and special recreation opportunities are available.

Peach Kuchen

serves 12

1/2 cup butter
2 cups flour (1-1/2 cup white, 1/2 cup whole
      wheat)
1/4 tsp. baking powder
1/2 tsp. salt
1/2 cup half-and-half
1/2 cup sour cream
3/4 cup brown sugar
12 peach halves or equal amount of sliced
      peaches*
3 whole eggs
2 tsp. cinnamon

Cut butter into flour, baking powder, salt, and 2 Tb. of the
sugar with pastry cutter until it appears as a coarse meal.
Press firmly into baking pan. Arrange peaches on surface to
cover. Sprinkle fruit with mixture of cinnamon and remaining
sugar.

Bake at 400° for 15 minutes. Pour eggs, beaten with half-
and-half and sour cream over top and bake 35 minutes
longer at 350°.

*You may use other fruit. The Grand Old House enjoys
 Rhubarb Kuchen!

Recipe offered by Cyndy DeBruler.

The Grand Old House

Rhubarb Coffee Cake

1/2 cup butter
1-1/2 cups sugar
1 egg, beaten
1 tsp. vanilla
2 cups flour
1 tsp. baking soda
1/2 tsp. salt
1 cup buttermilk
2 cups chopped rhubarb, floured
1/2 cup sugar
1 tsp. cinnamon
1/4 cup butter

Cream butter and 1-1/2 cups sugar. Add egg and vanilla and beat well. Sift flour, baking soda and salt together, adding alternately with buttermilk to creamed mixture. Gently blend in rhubarb. Pour into a greased 9x13-inch baking dish.

Mix remaining 1/2 cup sugar with cinnamon and 1/4 cup butter until crumbly. Sprinkle over batter. Bake at 350° for 35 minutes.

Chris Weseman, Hood River

Sally's Danish Puff

First layer:
1 cup flour
1/2 cup butter
2 Tb. water

Second layer:
1/2 cup butter
1 cup boiling water
1 tsp. almond flavoring
1 cup flour
3 eggs

Frosting:
powdered sugar
butter
milk
almond extract
chopped almonds

For the first layer, cut flour into butter. Sprinkle with water, mix with a fork. Roll into a ball and divide in half. Pat each ball into a rectangle 5 x12-inches and place it on a slightly greased jelly roll pan. Repeat with other ball, making sure pastries do not touch.

For the second layer, bring to a boil 1 cup water and 1/2 cup butter. Add almond flavoring. Remove from the stove, and stir in flour gradually to keep from lumping. When smooth, add eggs, one at a time, beating with an electric beater each time until smooth. Divide in half and spread evenly on the first pastry layer. Bake at 350° for 30 to 40 minutes.

Frost with powdered sugar frosting and sprinkle with nuts.

Contributed by Sarah Larson , compliments of Sally Havig , White Salmon

A gracious Country Inn since 1937, **Inn of the White Salmon** *is recognized nationwide for its spectacular breakfasts.*

Bill, Loretta and Julie Hopper make a special effort to offer their guests ultimate service. Loretta, with the aid of two bakers, assembles and bakes about 35 different pastries fresh each day. Egg dishes are the next course.

Breakfast isn't all that draws visitors to the Inn. From many of the 19 rooms, guests have a view of Mt. Hood and the Columbia River. The Inn and all rooms are furnished with antiques, another true delight to make your stay at Inn of the White Salmon a memorable one.

201

Apricot Jam Strudel

Dough:
1 cup butter
2 cups plus 3 Tb. flour
1/2 tsp. salt
1 cup sour cream

Filling:
3/4 of an 18 ounce jar of apricot jam
1/2 cup white raisins
3/4 cup shredded coconut
2/3 cup chopped walnuts

powdered sugar

Cut the butter into the flour and salt until the mixture resembles coarse meal. Blend in sour cream. Refrigerate the dough two to three hours or overnight.

Bring dough to room temperature and cut into thirds. Roll each part to a 10x15-inch rectangle. Spread the jam over the three pieces; sprinkle the coconut, white raisins and nuts on top. Roll in jellyroll fashion. Pinch the seam and ends together.

Place on greased cookie sheet and bake at 350° for 25 to 30 minutes until lightly browned. Cool for 10 minutes, dust with powdered sugar, slice and serve warm.

Recipe offered by Loretta Hopper.

Dutch Babies

1/3 cup butter
4 eggs
1 cup flour
1/2 tsp. salt
1 Tb. sugar, optional
1 cup milk

fresh fruit in season, preserves or real maple
*   syrup*

Melt butter in a 9 x 13-inch baking dish. Mix in blender: eggs, flour and milk. Pour into baking dish. Bake at 400° for 20 minutes.

Serve with fresh fruit, preserves, or syrup. May be sprinkled with powdered sugar.

Wonderful for a Sunday morning breakfast and easy for a crowd.

We have seen this recipe many different ways, including having ingredients all at room temperature and a cold pan. This recipe does not require that, yet it creates a big, puffy Dutch Baby!

Joan Lynch, Hood River

Horse Thief Pancakes

makes 15 4-inch pancakes

2 eggs, separated
1-1/2 cups buttermilk
3 Tb. oil
1-1/2 cup flour
1-1/2 Tb. sugar
1-1/2 tsp. baking powder
3/4 tsp. baking soda
3/4 tsp. salt

Mix egg yolks and buttermilk. Add oil and stir. Mix all dry
ingredients together. Add flour mixture to buttermilk mixture.
Beat egg whites until stiff and then fold into batter. Cook on hot,
greased griddle, turning pancakes only once.

==============================

*Horse Thief Lake State Park is located at the edge of the Columbia
River east of Dallesport on the Washington side. It is surrounded
by rock formations where ancient Indian petroglyphs can be seen.
Also a great stopping place for swimming, boating and camping.*

Waffles

2 eggs, separated
2 cups buttermilk
1/4 cup melted butter
2 cups flour
1 tsp. salt
1-1/4 tsp. soda
3/4 tsp. baking powder

Mix batter the same as for pancakes. Use 1/3 to 1/2 cup batter
on hot, greased waffle iron. Cook as desired.

Peaceful Pastures Llama Ranch

Jerry and Rebeka Stone invite you to an atmosphere of serenity and beauty at **Llama Ranch Bed and Breakfast.**

Guests are encouraged to walk a llama around the 97 acre ranch or take a day long hike, where a panoramic view of Mt. Adams or Mt. Hood await. Five guest rooms are available as well as kitchen and laundry facilities.

The Stones would like you to be their special guests at 1980 Hwy 141, White Salmon and share the love of llamas with them!

Cornmeal Pancakes

1 cup boiling water
3/4 cup cornmeal

1 Tb. molasses
1 cup sour milk*
2 eggs

1-1/2 cups flour
1-1/2 tsp. salt
3 tsp. baking powder
1/4 tsp. soda
3 Tb. butter, melted

In a large bowl pour boiling water over cornmeal and stir until thick. Add molasses, sour milk and eggs. Beat well. Add flour, salt, baking powder and soda. Mix. Stir in melted butter.

Fry on a hot, greased griddle.

Cornmeal Pancakes are heavier than standard pancakes, and very filling!

* To sour sweet milk, have it at 70°. Place 1 Tb. lemon juice or white vinegar in the bottom of a 1 cup measuring cup and then fill it with fresh sweet milk. Stir and let the mixture stand for 5 minutes. You may also substitute buttermilk in recipes that call for sour milk.

Compliments of Rebeka Stone and Peaceful Pastures Llama Ranch

Potato Pancakes

2 pounds potatoes
1 medium onion
1/2 cup boiling water
3 eggs
1/3 cup flour
1 tsp. salt
1/2 tsp. baking powder
1/4 tsp. pepper
oil for frying

applesauce or sour cream

Shred potatoes in food processor (or by hand). Remove 2 cups. Shred onion. Add the onion to the two cups of potatoes. Strain off liquid. Put potato mixture in a large bowl and pour boiling water over it. Mix well. Beat in eggs, flour, salt, baking powder, pepper and reserved potatoes.

In a large skillet, heat about 1/2-inch of oil. Drop batter by the tablesoonful, a few at a time into the oil. Fry until golden, turning once, for about 5 minutes. Drain on paper towel. May be kept warm in a 200° oven.

Top with applesauce or sour cream if desired.

b
r
e
a
k
f
a
s
t
&
b
r
u
n
c
h

Fried Potatoes

serves 3 to 4

3 Tb. safflower oil
3 large potatoes, diced
8 mushroons, sliced
4 green onions, chopped
salt and pepper to taste
1 Tb. parsley
paprika
1 cup Monterey Jack or Mozzarella cheese,
    grated

In a large skillet, heat oil and cook potatoes until tender. * Add mushrooms and green onion, salt and pepper. Continue cooking until potatoes are brown. Sprinkle with paprika and parsley. Add cheese and cover until melted.

*You may also add 1/2 cup carrots, celery, onion, or green pepper. Add these 5 minutes before adding mushrooms and green onion.

The Only Granola

10 cups rolled oats
2 cups nuts - sunflower seeds or chopped
     almonds or walnuts*
1 cup honey
1-1/4 cups butter
1 cup bran
1-1/2 Tb. cinnamon
1-1/2 Tb. vanilla
raisins, optional

Mix all ingredients together. Put into 2 greased 9x13-inch pans and bake at 350° for 20 minutes. Stir and bake 15 minutes more.

* Jan prefers almonds and no raisins

Jan Merz, Parkdale

Mimi's Cooked Breakfast Cereal

4 cups rolled oats
2 cups rolled triticale
2 cups rolled rye
2 cups rolled wheat
2 cups rolled barley
2 cups oat bran
1 cup wheat germ
1 cup sunflower seeds
1 cup sesame seeds
1 cup bran flakes
2 cups raisins
2 Tb. allspice
2 Tb. cinnamon

Mix all together in a GIGANTIC, ENORMOUS, HUGE bowl. Store in covered cannisters or gallon jars.

For 1 serving:
Bring to a boil, in medium saucepan, 1 cup water. Reduce heat to very low and stir in 1/3 cup mixture. Cover and simmer for 10 to 20 minutes, depending on desired consistency.

Serve plain or with honey. A very substantial cereal that will fill you up until lunch!

Microwave instructions:
Microwave in a glass bowl covered with a plate on high for 4 minutes. Let set for 5 minutes to finish cooking.

All ingredients are available locally at Wy'East Naturals.

Mimi Macht, Hood River

The Williams House Inn is a large gracious Victorian home, in a picture-book setting. The interior is furnished with Georgian and Victorian antiques and with a collection of early Chinese objects d'art.

Hosts Don and Barbara Williams graciously invite you into their home and will share with you a broad knowledge of the area and its history.

Bing Cherry Bowl

1 can Bing cherries
1/4 cup port wine

Drain cherries, reserving 1/4 cup juice. Combine reserved juice, port wine and cherries. Chill and serve.

Orange Delight

1/2 orange
1 Tb. plain yogurt
warm Seville orange marmalade

Peel and slice orange. Remove white membrane. Spoon yogurt and then marmalade over the top.

These recipes were offered by Barbara Williams, The Williams House Inn.

breakfast & brunch

Williams House Inn
Est. 1899

212

Grace's Bartlett Pear Pudding

serves 4

3 cups canned pears, drained
3 Tb. ground raw almonds
8 tsp. dry milk
1/8 tsp. almond extract

Put above ingredients in a blender and blend until smooth. Chill.

Wonderful breakfast with bran muffins!

Grace Wenger, Mt. Hood

breakfast & brunch

Orchard Hill Baked Pears

Wash pears and core to within 1-inch of the bottom. **Bartlett, Anjous, or Bosc** *are best. Cut a hairline circle around middle of each pear through its skin.*

Fill pear centers with **brown sugar, nutmeg or mace, cinnamon, nuts, raisins, and butter.**

Put pears into a baking pan with 1-inch of water. Bake about 45 minutes. Baste with 1 Tb. cooking liquid.

Remove pears to a serving dish. Top with **cream, whipped cream or plain yogurt.**

Recipe offered by Orchard Hill Inn.

213

Early Risers

24 rolls

2 cups milk
1/3 cup sugar
1/3 cup vegetable oil
1 egg, beaten
2 tsp. salt
2 tsp. baking powder

2 Tb. dry yeast
1/2 cup warm water
5 to 6 cups flour

butter
granulated or brown sugar
cinnamon
nuts
raisins

Icing:
1/2 cup powdered sugar
1 to 2 Tb. milk

Scald the milk. Add the sugar, oil, egg, salt and baking powder. In a separate bowl; dissolve the yeast in warm water. Combine the yeast mixture with the warm milk mixture. Add flour and knead 5 to 10 minutes.

Place in greased bowl and cover. Let rise 1-1/2 hours. Punch down and divide in half. Roll each to a 12x14-inch rectangle. Spread with soft butter and sprinkle with sugar, cinnamon, nuts and raisins. Roll up and cut in 1-inch slices.

Space rolls 2-inches apart in lightly greased baking pans. Cover tightly with foil and refrigerate overnight. In the morning, remove from refrigerator 10 minutes before baking. Bake at 350° for 30 to 35 minutes.

Drizzle icing on rolls while hot. Enjoy!

Georgine Winn, Anchorage, Alaska

Almond-Cheese Coffeecake

serves 6 to 8

Dough:
1 Tb. yeast
1/4 cup water
2-1/2 cups flour
2 Tb. sugar
1/2 tsp. salt
6 Tb. cold butter
2 egg yolks
1/2 cup milk

Cheese Filling:
8 ounces cream cheese
1/4 cup sugar
3 Tb. flour
1 egg yolk
1 tsp. lemon peel
1 tsp. almond extract
1/4 cup sliced almonds

Glaze:
1/2 cup powdered
  sugar
1/4 tsp. vanilla
2 Tb. milk

Combine yeast and water. Let stand 5 minutes to soften. In a large bowl combine 2 cups flour, sugar, and salt. Cut in butter. Stir in yeast mixture, egg yolks and milk. Mix at medium speed to blend. Stir in 1/2 cup more flour to form a soft dough. Shape into a ball. Place in greased bowl, turning to coat top. Cover with plastic and chill 6 hours or overnight.

Punch dough down; turn onto a floured board. Roll dough into a 10x13-inch rectangle. Transfer to baking sheet. Spread filling to within 1-inch of edge, sprinkle with almonds. Roll dough jellyroll style to center of rectangle. Repeat for other side.

Make cuts through 1 roll at a time 1-1/2 inches apart, cutting to center. Gently lift and turn pieces on their sides to expose filling.

Cover and let rise until puffy, about 45 minutes. Bake at 350° for 25 minutes. Combine glaze ingredients and drizzle over coffee cake.

Schoolhouse Coffeecake

This is a favorite with the Macht family!

Cake:
3 cups flour
1 cup sugar
3 Tb. baking powder
1 cup milk
2 eggs
2 to 3 cups sliced apples, peaches, blueberries,
  or other fruit
3 Tb. butter, melted

Topping:
2/3 cup flour
2/3 cup brown sugar
2 tsp. cinnamon
6 Tb. butter, melted

Combine all the cake ingredients together in a large bowl.
Mix gently. Pour into a greased 9x13-inch baking pan.

Mix together topping ingredients and sprinkle topping over
cake.

Bake for 45 minutes at 375°.

Mimi Macht, Hood River

Kolåcky

makes 80

1 pound margarine or butter
1 pound cream cheese, room temperature
1 pound flour, about 3 cups

"Solo" apricot, poppyseed or prune filling*

powdered sugar

Mix butter and cream cheese together. Add flour, blending with <u>hands</u>. Refrigerate overnight.

Remove dough from refrigerator, cut in half, refrigerating other half until ready to use.

On lightly floured board, roll dough out 1/4- inch thick. Cut with a 2-inch round cookie or doughnut cutter. Place side-by-side on jelly roll pan or cookie sheet, and fill with 1/2 tsp. Solo filling. Repeat with other half. Bake at 375° for 25 minutes, until golden. Sprinkle with powdered sugar.

* Solo filling is available in the baking-supply section of most supermarkets.

An Easter special each year from Cheryl's mother, Helen Vik

Snow-Capped Yummy Buns

1 cup scalded sour cream
1/2 cup melted butter
1/2 cup sugar
1 tsp. salt
2 packages yeast
1/2 cup warm water
2 eggs, beaten
4 cups flour

Mix first 4 ingredients together and cool. Dissolve the yeast in the water and let sit until it bubbles. Combine the sour cream mixture, yeast mixture, and eggs. Blend. Add flour and mix well. Cover and refrigerate overnight.

After refrigerating, knead 4 to 5 times. Divide in 4 equal pieces. Roll each piece on a floured board into a 12x18- inch rectangle. Spread 1/4 of the filling on rolled out dough leaving a 1/2- inch margin. Roll up jellyroll style and pinch ends closed. Cut with sharp knife into 1-1/2-inch slices and place cut side down on cookie sheet. Repeat with remaining 3 pieces of dough. Cover and let rise 1-1/2 hours. Bake at 375° for 12 minutes or until golden brown. Drizzle glaze over buns while warm.

Cream Cheese Filling:
2 8 ounce packages cream cheese
3/4 cup sugar
1 egg
2 tsp. vanilla
1/2 tsp. salt

Glaze:
2 cups powdered sugar
1/4 cup milk

Stir together to make a thin frosting.

Don't let the number of ingredients fool you! These buns are remarkably easy to make, especially since the dough is made the night before and requires no kneading.

Breads

Dills

Oneonta Falls French Bread

2 loaves

2-1/4 cups water
2 Tb. yeast
7 to 7-1/2 cups unbleached white flour
1-1/2 tsp. salt
1 egg, beaten with 1 Tb. water
2 Tb. sesame seeds

Dissolve yeast in water. Add salt to flour, then gradually add to water/yeast mixture, one cup at a time. Knead on a lightly floured board for 8 to10 minutes, until smooth and elastic.

Place dough in oiled bowl, turning to coat. Cover and let rise until doubled, about 1 hour. Punch down and let rise again, about 45 minutes.

Turn out onto a lightly floured board and divide into 2 portions. Roll each out into a 12x20- inch rectangle. Roll up tightly, beginning at long side, sealing well as you go.

Place each loaf diagonally, seam side down, on a greased baking sheet that has been sprinkled lightly with cornmeal. With a sharp knife, gash tops diagonally every 3-inches, about 1/4 inch deep. Brush on egg wash. Sprinkle with sesame seeds.

Let rise until doubled, about 40 minutes. Bake at 350° for 20 to 30 minutes, until golden brown and crusty. Cool.

b
r
e
a
d

Oneonta Gorge is a cool, mossy, narrow canyon that has a unique botanical area inhabited by plants that like moisture and shade. Follow the gorge to the falls and beyond, joining other trails for loop hikes.

Tamanawas Falls Brown Bread

I tsp. sugar
2-1/2 cups water
I Tb. yeast
1/4 cup oil
1/2 cups molasses
4 cups whole wheat flour
4 to 5 cups all-purpose flour
I Tb. salt
I Tb. wheat germ
I Tb. caraway seeds

bread

To 2-1/2 cups warm water, add yeast and sugar and let sit 5
minutes to proof. Add oil and molasses. Stir in 4 cups whole
wheat flour, 1 Tb. salt and 4 cups all-purpose flour. Beat well,
knead until smooth and elastic. Add 1 Tb. wheat germ and 1 Tb.
caraway seeds while kneading dough. Add one more cup flour
if needed. Let rise until double. Punch down and let rise again.
Form into 4 round loaves. Let rise for 30 minutes. Bake at 400°
for 5 minutes. Reduce heat to 375° and continue to bake for one
hour.

_____

*To reach Tamanawas Falls, travel 11 miles south of the community
of Mt. Hood on Hwy 35. At Sherwood Campground, follow the
tranquil 1.5 mile foot trail up to the falls. Many times during the
year you can walk behind the waterfall for an unusual perspective.*

English Muffin Bread

1 package active dry yeast
1 Tb. granulated sugar
1/2 cup warm water
2-1/2 cups flour
2 tsp. salt
7/8 cup warm milk
1/4 tsp. baking soda dissolved in 1 Tb. warm
    water

Combine the yeast, sugar and warm water in a large bowl, stir until the yeast and sugar are dissolved. Let mixture sit until it bubbles. Add the flour, mixed with the salt, and the warm milk in alternate portions while stirring with a wooden spoon. Beat the dough until it shows some elasticity and almost leaves the sides of the bowl (it will still be gummy). Cover and let rise in a warm place for 1-1/2 hours, or until doubled in size.

Stir down and add the soda mixture. Beat vigorously for about 1 minute. Place dough in one buttered 10-inch or two 8x4x2-inch bread pans. Let rise again for about 1 hour. Bake at 375° until golden. Cool in the pans for about 5 minutes, then turn out onto racks.

Excellent when sliced and toasted!

Pita Bread

2 packages active dry yeast
1/4 tsp. sugar
2 cups warm water
1/4 cup olive oil
1-1/2 Tb. salt
6 cups all-purpose flour, or hard-wheat flour
cornmeal

Dissolve yeast and sugar in 1/2 cup warm water in a large mixing bowl and allow to proof, about 5 minutes. Add remaining 1-1/2 cups warm water, oil, salt and 5 cups flour, mixing vigorously, one cup at a time. The dough should be sticky. Turn out on to a floured board and work in the remaining flour if necessary. Knead for 10 minutes or until the dough is smooth and elastic. Shape into a ball, place in a buttered bowl, and turn to coat. Cover and let rise in a warm place for 1-1/2 to 2 hours, or until doubled in size.

Punch down dough and allow to rest for 10 minutes. Divide into eight equal pieces and shape each into a ball. Cover and let rest for 30 minutes. Flatten each ball with a well-floured rolling pin and roll to 1/8-inch thickness in 8-inch circles. Dust two baking sheets with cornmeal, place two circles of dough on each, cover and let rest for 30 minutes. (Leave remaining circles on floured board until first are baked.)

Preheat the oven to 500°. Put one of the baking sheets on the lower rack of the oven for 5 minutes. Do not open the oven door until the five minutes are up. Transfer the sheet to a higher shelf and continue to bake for 3 to 5 minutes longer until puffy and lightly browned. Repeat with remaining baking sheet and additional dough rounds.

b
r
e
a
d

Pinnacle Peak Damper Bread

1 loaf

1 Tb. dry yeast
1/4 cup warm water
1 cup milk, room temperature
3 to 4 cups unbleached flour
1 Tb. baking powder
3/4 tsp. salt
2 Tb. butter

Stir yeast into water, let set 5 minutes to proof.

Stir in milk and set aside. Mix dry ingredients together. Cut butter into flour mixture with a pastry blender. Pour in milk mixture all at once and stir until the dough holds together.

Turn dough out onto a lightly floured board and knead (about 20 times) until smooth, adding a bit more flour, if needed. Shape into 1 round loaf and cut a deep X across top of loaf. Dust lightly with flour. Place in a greased round pan. Bake at 375° on bottom rack in oven about 45 to 55 minutes. Remove from pan and let cool on a rack for 10 minutes, serve while warm.

b
r
e
a
d

223

Early Morning Buns

makes 6 dozen

<u>4:30 to 6:30 pm</u>

1 package active dry yeast
1 Tb. sugar
1/2 cup warm water

1/2 cup oil
1/2 cup sugar

4 eggs, beaten
2 cups warm water
1 Tb. salt
10 cups flour (may use 1/2 whole wheat, 1/2
    white)

In a large bowl, stir yeast and sugar into 1/2 cup warm water
and let stand until bubbly, about 10 minutes. Add oil and
sugar. Mix well. Add eggs, water, salt, and 1 cup flour. Beat
well. Add remaining flour to make a stiff mixture without
being too sticky. Knead and form into a ball. Cover and let
rise until 10 pm.

Punch down and form into golf ball-size buns and place,
sides just touching, on greased cookie sheets. Cover and
let rise at room temperature overnight.

Bake at 350° for 15 to 20 minutes, until golden.

Sandy Henderson, Lumsden, Canada

Andrew's Pizza and Bakery

Andrew's Pizza & Bakery is located on Oak Street in Hood River and features the finest scones, muffins and breads baked fresh every morning. Available by the slice are homemade, hand-tossed pizzas with a choice of gourmet toppings and can be enjoyed with microbrews on tap.

Honey Oat Bread

8 cups bread flour
1 1/2 cups quick cooking oats
1 1/2 Tbs. salt
3 cups warm water
1 Tb. yeast
1 1/2 Tbs. sugar
1/2 cup honey
1/4 cup molasses

Combine first 3 ingredients in bowl or mixer with dough hook. Whisk together sugar and warm water and gradually stir in yeast. Let sit until foamy on top.

Add yeast mixture to flour and oats. Pour honey and molasses on top and mix all together adding flour as necessary. Knead for 8 to10 minutes. Let rise in warm place until double in size.

Punch down, divide and form into 2 loaves. Place in greased loaf pans. Let rise until double.

Bake at 350° for 20 to 25 minutes.

Recipe offered by Andrew and Melissa

b
r
e
a
d

Ellen's Beer Bread

3 cups flour
3-3/4 tsp. baking powder
2-1/4 tsp. salt
3 Tb. sugar
1 bottle warm beer
touch of water
1 to 2 tsp. dry onion, optional
1/2 tsp. dill weed, optional
1 tsp. rosemary, optional

Mix all ingredients together. Pour into greased loaf pan.
Bake at 375° for 1 hour.

A very easy bread to make. Serve with soup, chili or salad.

Ellen Larsen, Hood River

b
r
e
a
d

Helen's No-Knead Herb Bread

1-1/2 cups whole wheat flour
1/4 cup sugar
1 Tb. instant minced onion
1 to 1-1/2 tsp. garlic salt
1 to 1-1/2 tsp. Italian seasoning
2 Tb. active dry yeast
1 cup water
1 cup milk
1/4 cup oil
1 egg
2-1/2 to 3 cups unbleached flour

Combine first six ingredients in a large mixing bowl. Heat water, milk and oil over low heat until warm. Add egg and warm liquid to flour mixture. Blend at low speed until moistened. Continue beating 3 more minutes at medium speed. Gradually stir in unbleached flour to form a stiff batter.

Cover dough; let rise in warm place until double in size. Stir down. Spoon into a 2-quart buttered casserole or a buttered 9 x 13-inch pan.

Bake at 375° for 45 to 50 minutes or until loaf sounds hollow when tapped. Remove from pan to cool. Brush with butter and coarse salt if desired.

A favorite recipe from a special neighbor, Helen Bellinger, Mt. Hood.

b
r
e
a
d

Stonehenge Rolls

20 rolls

6 cups unbleached flour
2 Tb. yeast
1 Tb. sugar
1 tsp. salt
2 Tb. butter
2-1/4 cups water (105° to 115°)
salad oil

Put 2 cups of the flour, yeast, sugar, salt and butter in large bowl. Add water all at once and beat with electric mixer for 2 minutes. Add 1 more cup flour and beat 1 more minute until thick and elastic. With wooden spoon, stir in the remaining flour, knead for 5 minutes. Shape into a ball, cover and let rest for 20 minutes.

Divide the dough into 20 to 24 equal portions, each about the size of a large egg. Shape into an oval. Put these on greased cookie sheets.

Brush rolls lightly with oil, cover with plastic wrap and refrigerate for 2 to 24 hours.

When ready to bake, preheat oven to 400°. Remove rolls from refrigerator, uncover, and slash rolls 1/4-inch deep down the center. Brush gently with cold water. Bake rolls for 20 minutes or until golden.

Compliments of Mimi Macht, Hood River

b
r
e
a
d

===

Eastern end of the Columbia Gorge points of interest include the site of ancient petroglyphs near Wishram; the Maryhill Museum with a magnificent view of the gorge, plus one of the nation's finest collections of the work of French sculptor Auguste Rodin, and displays of Indian Artifacts; the Goldendale Observatory; and a replica of Stonehenge, the Druid temple on the plains of Salisbury in southern England.

Bran Muffin Bread

1 large and 1 small loaf

3 eggs
3/4 cup oil
1/2 cup brown sugar
1 cup white sugar
3 tsp. vanilla

1 cup whole wheat flour
1 cup all-purpose flour
1/4 cup soy flour
1/4 cup cracked wheat
1/2 tsp. baking powder
1 tsp. salt
2 tsp. baking soda
1/2 cup wheat germ

2 cups shredded zucchini or apple
1 cup sunflower seeds

1/3 cup sesame seeds

Beat first five ingredients together. Combine dry ingredients (next 8 ingredients) and add to egg mixture. Fold in zucchini and sunflower seeds. Pour into 1 large well-greased loaf pan and 1 small loaf pan. Sprinkle with sesame seeds and bake at 350° for 50 minutes until center is done.

Jeanne Gaulke, Hood River

bread

Bartlett Pear Nut Bread

makes 3 loaves

2 to 3 fresh Hood River Valley Bartlett Pears
3 eggs
1 cup oil
1 cup sugar
1/2 tsp. lemon peel, grated
1 tsp. vanilla
3 cups flour
1 tsp. salt
1 tsp. baking soda
1/4 tsp. baking powder
1-1/2 tsp. cinnamon
2/3 cup chopped nuts

Coarsely grate pears to make 2 cups. Beat eggs until light and fluffy. Add oil, sugar, lemon peel, vanilla and grated pear. Mix thoroughly. Sift together dry ingredients and add to pear mixture, mixing until blended. Stir in nuts. Pour batter into 3 greased 7-1/2 x 3-1/2 x 2-inch loaf pans. Bake at 325° for 50 to 60 minutes or until bread tests done.

Jan Merz, Parkdale

Pear Bread

2 cups buttermilk biscuit mix
1/2 cup sugar
1/2 tsp. baking soda
2 fresh pears, peeled and puréed
1/2 tsp. salt
2 beaten eggs
1/2 cup sour cream
1/2 cup chopped walnuts

Mix well the biscuit mix, sugar, baking soda and salt. Add the puréed pears. Combine beaten eggs and sour cream. Add to pear mixture. Mix well. Stir in walnuts. Bake in a greased 9 x 5-inch loaf pan for 50 minutes, or until done.

Laura L. Young, Hood River

230

b
r
e
a
d

Hood River Valley
Pear Tea Bread

1 cup fresh pears (2 or 3)
1/2 cup salad oil
2 eggs, slightly beaten (or 3 egg whites)
1/2 cup sugar or 3/8 cup honey
2 tsp. lemon rind, grated
2 cups whole wheat flour
1/2 cup all-purpose flour
1 Tb. baking powder
3/4 tsp. salt
1/4 tsp. ground cardamon

1/2 cup chopped walnuts
1/2 cup raisins (optional)

Peel, core and purée pears. Add the oil, eggs, sugar or honey and lemon rind.

Stir together the dry ingredients and mix together with the pear mixture. Stir in walnuts and raisins.

Bake at 350° in a greased 8-1/2 x 4-1/2-inch loaf pan for 50 to 55 minutes. Let cool in pan for 5 minutes, turn out onto wire rack.

A firm, not-too-sweet bread. . . perfect with a fruit salad, or served warm for dessert with lemon sauce! (see page 321)

Mary Schlick, Mt. Hood

bread

Mavis' Pumpkin Bread

3-1/2 cups flour
2 tsp. baking powder
1/2 tsp. baking soda
1-1/2 tsp. salt
1 tsp. cinnamon
1/2 tsp. cloves
4 eggs
2-2/3 cups sugar
1 14 ounce can pumpkin
1 cup water
1/2 cup oil
2/3 cup chopped walnuts
2/3 cup raisins

Combine dry ingredients. In medium bowl beat eggs, sugar, pumpkin, water and oil. Make a well in middle of dry ingredients and add liquid mixture all at once. Mix only enough to moisten, making sure there is no visible flour. Mix in raisins and nuts. Pour into greased and floured loaf pans. Bake at 350° for one hour. Cool completely. Store in refrigerator. This bread freezes beautifully.

A wonderful Canadian recipe from Mavis Frederickson.

Swedish Lefse

2 pounds russet potatoes
2 cups flour
salt

Boil potatoes in skins. Cool slightly, peel and rice or mash. Refrigerate uncovered until cold. Remove from refrigerator and mix together with flour and about 1/2 tsp. salt, or to taste. Form into meatball-size balls. You may refrigerate again at this point. Roll out on well floured board until very thin. Cook on hot, well seasoned grill a few minutes on each side. Cool briefly, and stack. Store in an airtight container and refrigerate.

Compliments of Helen Vik

Lefse is traditionally served on Christmas Eve, rolled up with butter and eaten with Lutefisk and potato sausage. However, it is wonderful on Thanksgiving with turkey and cranberry sauce, or any time of the year as an alternative to rolls, bread or tortillas. Lefse gets easier to make every time and is always a treat.

b
r
e
a
d

Angel Biscuits

makes 24 to 30

5 cups flour
1 tsp. baking soda
3 tsp. baking powder
1 tsp. salt
3 Tb. sugar
1 cup shortening
1 Tb. dry active yeast
2 Tb. warm water
2 cups buttermilk
melted butter

Mix flour, baking soda, baking powder, salt and sugar. Cut in shortening. Dissolve yeast in warm water; stir in buttermilk. Add to dry ingredients, mix lightly. Turn dough on to floured surface and shape into a smooth ball by hand. Don't knead. Roll out to thin rectangle; fold in half and roll again lightly to 1/4- inch thick.

Cut with biscuit cutter. Place biscuits on greased pan. Brush tops with melted butter. Let rise until light, about 4 hours. Bake at 450° for 12 to 15 minutes.

Dough will keep in refrigerator for several days.

Lois Sharkey, Mt. Hood

b
r
e
a
d

234

Almond Blueberry Muffins

makes 24 miniature

muffins

1/2 cup blanched almonds
1-1/2 cups flour
2 Tb. sugar
1/3 cup brown sugar
2 tsp. baking powder
1/4 tsp. salt
1/2 tsp cinnamon
2 eggs
1/2 cup buttermilk
1/3 cup water
2 Tb. butter, melted
1/2 tsp. almond extract
1 cup blueberries
1/4 cup sliced almonds

Grind whole almonds in blender until finely ground.
Combine almond powder, flour, sugars, baking powder, salt,
and cinnamon in a mixing bowl; set aside.

Process eggs, buttermilk, water, butter, and almond extract
in blender until smooth. Make a well in the center of dry
ingredients; pour in the liquid ingredients. Stir just until
moistened. Fold in the blueberries.

Spoon batter two-thirds full into greased miniature muffin
pans. Bake at 400° for 15 to 18 minutes.

b
r
e
a
d

ORCHARD HILL
INN

A secluded homestead overlooking the orchards and forested slopes of the White Salmon River Valley, Orchard Hill Inn. Hosts James and Pamela Tindall invite guests to the most secluded Bed and Breakfast in the Columbia Gorge.

In the mornings look forward to a delectably wholesome sideboard breakfast of fresh breads, cakes, cheeses, spreads, yogurt and homegrown fruit.

Three rooms, furnished with family treasures, photographs and locally made quilts are available.

Bird watchers, golfers, windsurfers and skiers will find a wide array of activities to fill a day, while staying at Orchard Hill Inn, located at 199 Oak Ridge Road in White Salmon.

Mt. Adams Sawtooth
Huckleberry Bran Muffins

12 muffins

1 cup unprocessed bran
1-1/2 cups whole wheat flour
1/2 cup Mt. Adams Sawtooth huckleberries
1/2 cup. walnut pieces
1 tsp. baking powder
1 tsp. baking soda
3/4 cup milk
2 Tb. oil
1 egg, beaten
1/2 cup molasses

Stir together bran, flour, baking soda, baking powder. Stir in huckleberries and walnuts. Set aside.

Blend together milk, molasses,oil, and egg. Add to dry ingredients and stir only until moistened.

Spoon into greased muffin tins and bake at 375° for 12 to 15 minutes.

Recipe offered by Orchard Hill Inn.

bread

Kitsy's Bran Muffins

makes 16

1-1/2 cups bran, unprocessed
1-1/3 cups whole wheat flour
1/4 cup brown sugar
1/2 tsp. salt, optional
2-1/2 tsp. baking soda
2 eggs, slightly beaten
1 cup buttermilk
1/2 cup oil
1/3 cup molasses
1/3 cup honey
1 cup raisins

Combine bran, flour, sugar, salt and baking soda. Add eggs, buttermilk, oil, molasses and honey. Stir with a wire whisk just until all ingredients are blended. Add raisins. Bake at 425° in greased muffin tins for 10 to 12 minutes.

For a low calorie recipe, omit the brown sugar and reduce oil to 1/4 cup.

Kitsy Stanley, Mt. Hood

Max's Ripe Banana Muffins

makes 15 to 18

2 to 3 bananas
6 Tb. oil
1 egg
1/2 cup brown sugar
1/2 tsp. salt
1 tsp. vanilla
1-1/2 cups flour
1 tsp. baking soda
1 tsp. baking powder
1/2 cup chopped nuts
1/2 cup raisins

Put oil and egg in blender. Slice bananas into mixture and blend until smooth. Stir in sugar, salt and vanilla. Mix dry ingredients together. Add to banana mixture, add nuts and raisins and stir until just blended.

Spoon into greased muffin pans and bake at 350° for 18 to 20 minutes.

Maxine Wahl, Lumsden, Canada

bread

239

Cape Horn Morning Muffins

makes 1 dozen

2 cups flour
1/2 cup white sugar
1/2 cup brown sugar
2 tsp. cinnamon
1/4 tsp. salt
2 tsp. baking soda

2 cups grated carrots
1/2 cup raisins
1/2 cup coconut
1 Newtown apple, grated

3 eggs
3/4 cup salad oil
1 tsp. vanilla
1 tsp. lemon juice

b
r
e
a
d

In a large bowl combine first 6 ingredients. Stir in next 4 ingredients. Beat together eggs, oil, vanilla and lemon juice. Add it to the batter and stir until just combined. Spoon into well greased muffin cups, filling to the top. Bake at 350° for about 20 minutes.

================

On the Washington side of the Columbia River, Cape Horn Viewpoint offers an incredible photogenic view of the west entrance to the Gorge.

240

Shelley's Spiced Carrot Muffins

makes 12 muffins

1-1/2 cups flour
1 tsp. baking powder
1/2 tsp. salt
3/4 tsp. cinnamon
3/4 tsp. allspice
1/3 cup brown sugar
1 egg
2/3 cup buttermilk
1/4 cup oil
1-1/2 cups grated carrots
1/2 cup raisins
1/2 cup chopped nuts

Mix dry ingredients together in a bowl. Beat egg, buttermilk and oil. Stir in carrots, raisins and nuts. Pour into dry ingredients. Stir just until moist. Don't overmix. Fill lined muffin tins 2/3 full and bake at 400° for 15 to 17 minutes. Turn out while warm.

Shelley Lax, Lumsden, Canada

bread

Sugared Rhubarb Muffins

makes 24

2-1/2 cups flour
1-1/2 cups brown sugar
2/3 cup salad oil
1 egg slightly beaten
1 cup buttermilk
1/2 cup nuts (optional)
1 tsp. salt
1 tsp. baking soda
1 tsp. vanilla
2-1/2 cups chopped rhubarb

Combine all ingredients and mix just until blended.

Pour 2/3 full into paper lined or greased muffin tins. Sprinkle topping evenly over each muffin.

Topping:
1/2 cup finely chopped walnuts
1/2 cup sugar
1 Tb. butter
1 tsp. cinnamon

Combine all ingredients for topping.

Bake at 400° for 25 minutes.

b
r
e
a
d

Sweet Jammy Muffins

makes 1 dozen

2 cups flour
1/4 cup sugar
1 Tb. baking powder
1/2 tsp. baking soda
1/2 tsp. salt
1/4 cup butter
1 cup yogurt
1/4 cup milk
1 egg
1/2 tsp. vanilla
1/4 cup raspberry preserves
powdered sugar

Blend dry ingredients in bowl. Melt butter, remove from heat and stir in yogurt and milk. When smooth, beat in egg and vanilla. Add butter mixture to dry ingredients and stir well.

Spoon half the batter into buttered muffin tins. Place about a tsp. of jam over batter in each cup and top with remaining batter.

Bake at 425° for 15 to 20 minutes until golden. Let stand 5 minutes before removing from tin. Sift a little powdered sugar over muffins before serving.

Jackie Frost, Parkdale

b
r
e
a
d

Chocolate Chip Muffins

makes 1 dozen

1-1/2 cups all-purpose flour or
half whole wheat
1/2 cup sugar
2 Tb. honey
3 tsp. baking powder
1/8 tsp. salt
1 cup milk
1 egg
1 cup chocolate chips

Mix together dry ingredients; add chocolate chips.

Combine honey, egg, milk and butter; stir into flour mixture until blended. Spoon into paper lined or well greased muffin cups, filling 2/3 full.

Bake at 375° for 18 to 20 minutes. Serve warm.

b
r
e
a
d

Chelan and Barkley's Favorite Dog Biscuits

2 cups whole wheat flour
1/2 cup rye flour
1/2 cup brewers yeast
1 cup bulgur
1/2 cup cornmeal
1/4 cup parsley flakes
1/4 cup dry milk
1 tsp. dry yeast
1/4 cup warm water
1 cup chicken broth
1 egg, beaten with 1 Tb. milk

Combine flours, brewers yeast, bulgur, cornmeal, parsley, and dry milk in a large bowl. In a small bowl combine dry yeast and warm water. Stir until yeast is dissolved. Add chicken broth. Stir liquid into dry ingredients, mixing well with hands. Dough will be very stiff. Roll out dough to 1/4-inch thickness. Cut with a bone-shaped cookie cutter. Transfer biscuits to cookie sheet and brush lightly with egg glaze.

Bake at 300° for 45 minutes. Turn off oven and let biscuits dry out in oven overnight.

Even the cats love these biscuits! Great to make for your special friend.

bread

Sweet Endings

Bingen Bakery

Bingen Bakery *has been owned and operated since 1985, by Mike and Pam Hughes. They pride themselves in the fact that all of their bakery products are made from scratch on the premises.*

In this custom bakery shop patrons are welcomed by friendly service and delicious aromas Tuesday through Saturday 4:30 am to 5:30 pm, located at 213 Steuben Avenue in Bingen.

Pam's Seltzer Cake

1-1/2 cups butter or margarine
3 cups sugar
5 eggs
3 cups flour
2 Tb. lemon extract
3/4 cup '7-up'

Cream together butter and sugar for 20 minutes. Add eggs (one at a time), flour and extract. Fold in '7-up'. Pour into a well-greased and floured 12-cup bundt pan. Bake at 325° for 1 to 1/4 hours.

Use your imagination with this delicious recipe. Substitute flavored seltzers and extracts, such as vanilla or almond.

Recipe offered by Pam Hughes, Bingen Bakery.

s
w
e
e
t

e
n
d
i
n
g

Lemon Cloud Cake

2 cups all purpose flour
1/2 tsp. salt
2-1/2 tsp. baking powder
1/3 cup instant dry milk
1-1/2 cups sugar
1/2 cup butter, softened
1 cup water
1 Tb. grated lemon rind
3 egg whites, beaten until stiff peaks form

Grease and flour 2 8-inch round layer cake pans. Sift flour, salt, baking powder, dry milk and sugar together into a large bowl. Add butter, water and rind. Beat 2 minutes at medium speed. Add egg whites and beat 2 minutes more. Pour batter into pans. Bake at 350° for 30 minutes or until done. Cool. Remove one cake from pan and place on serving plate. Spread with lemon cream within 1/2-inch from edge. Set remaining layer on top and frost.

Lemon Cream Filling:

2/3 cup powdered milk
1/2 cup sugar
3 egg yolks, beaten
1 Tb. grated lemon rind
2 Tb. cornstarch
1-1/4 cups water
2 Tb. butter
1/4 cup lemon juice

Mix dry milk, cornstarch, and sugar in saucepan. Stir in gradually until smooth, a mixture of water and the egg yolks. Cook and stir constantly over medium heat until it is thick and just begins to bubble. Lower heat and continue to cook for 2 minutes. Remove from heat and stir in lemon juice, rind and butter until smooth. Cool before spreading on cake.

Lemon Icing:

2 egg whites
3 Tb. cold water
1/4 tsp. cream of tartar
1-1/2 tsp. corn syrup
1-1/2 cups sugar
2 Tb. lemon juice
1/4 tsp. lemon rind

Place all ingredients in a double boiler over rapidly boiling water. Beat constantly with a rotary beater for 7 minutes, or 5 minutes with an electric mixer. Remove from heat. Add vanilla or lemon extract. Continue beating by hand if necessary until it reaches desired consistency.

Dorothy VonderBecke, Underwood

s
w
e
e
t

e
n
d
i
n
g

Lemon Cake

Cake:

1 package yellow cake mix
1 small package lemon jello or pudding
4 eggs
3/4 cup water
3/4 cup oil
1 tsp. lemon peel or zest

Beat together cake mix, jello, eggs, water, oil and lemon zest on medium speed for 4 minutes. Pour batter into greased and floured bundt pan. Bake at 350° for 50 to 60 minutes, or until cake is done.

Glaze:

2 tsp. lemon zest
1/4 cup lemon juice
1/4 cup sugar

Combine glaze ingredients. Poke holes in cake while still warm and in the pan and pour glaze over the cake. Cool 20 minutes.

Slice and eat plain or top with strawberries, blueberries, or peaches and whipped cream.

s
w
e
e
t

e
n
d
i
n
g

Walnut Torte

Cake:
3 cups flour
3/4 cup sugar
1/2 tsp. salt
1 cup butter
1 egg

Filling:
2 cups ground walnuts
1-1/2 cups powdered sugar
1 tsp. brandy
2 cups sour cream
1 tsp. vanilla
apricot preserves, strained
powdered sugar

Combine flour, sugar and salt in large mixing bowl. Cut the cold butter into this mixture with fingers. Add the egg and mix it in to form a ball. Divide ball of dough into 6 equal parts. Roll each part into a 9-inch circle and bake on the back sides of lightly floured 9-inch cake pans for 10 to12 minutes, or until edges are golden. Let layers cool and remove from the pans.

To prepare the filling: combine walnuts, sugar, brandy, sour cream and vanilla. Stir until smooth. Spread filling over each cake layer except the layer for the top. Press them together gently.

Spread the strained apricot preserves on the top of the cake and sprinkle with powdered sugar. Cut into thin wedges to serve.

A delightful torte for a special occasion!

Ina Lassen, Parkdale

The Fruit Tree

The Fruit Tree, owned and operated by the Betts family since 1984, is famous for seasonal local fruit. The beautiful new store, easily accessible from I-84, also offers gift packs, Northwest salmon, and Oregon jams, jellies, candy, and dried fruit. In addition, the visitor at the Fruit Tree will find an outstanding collection of garments from around the world.

Grandma's Applesauce Cake

s
w
e
e
t

e
n
d
i
n
g

2 cups applesauce, juicy
2 cups flour
2 eggs
2 Tbs. cocoa
1/2 tsp. salt
1/2 tsp. cinnamon
1/4 tsp. nutmeg
1/4 tsp. ginger
1/2 tsp. soda
1 Tbs. baking powder
1/2 cup shortening
2 cups sugar
1 cup nuts, chopped
1 cup raisins
1 cup chopped dates

Combine all ingredients in a large bowl. Mix gently and pour into a greased 9 x 13-inch pan. Bake at 300° until barely done, about 1 hour (just a bit underbaked is preferred).

Wedding Carrot Cake

1-3/4 cup flour
2 tsp. baking soda
1 tsp. baking powder
3 tsp. cinnamon
1/2 tsp. ginger
1 tsp. salt

1-1/4 cup oil
1-3/4 cup sugar
4 eggs

1 tsp. vanilla
1-3/4 cup grated carrot
3 ounces drained, crushed pineapple
1 cup coconut
1/2 cup nuts

Stir flour, baking soda, baking powder, cinnamon, ginger and salt together. Set aside. Beat together in mixing bowl the oil, sugar and eggs. Add the flour mixture and beat until combined. Add vanilla, carrots, pineapple, coconut and nuts. Pour into 3 round greased and floured cake pans.

Bake at 350° for 35 to 40 minutes. Test with a toothpick to see if done. Let cool in pans for 15 minutes. Turn out onto cake rack and cool completely. Make frosting.

Frosting:
1/2 cup butter
1 pound powdered sugar
8 ounces cream cheese, softened

Whip butter, powdered sugar and cream cheese together. Frost cake.

Marilyn's Chocolate Zucchini Cake

2-1/2 cups flour
1/4 cup cocoa
1 tsp. soda
1 tsp. salt
1/2 cup butter
1/2 cup oil
1-3/4 cups sugar
2 eggs
2 cups grated zucchini
1 tsp. vanilla
1/2 to 3/4 cup chocolate chips
1/2 to 3/4 cup chopped nuts
1/2 cup buttermilk

chocolate chips
chopped nuts

Sift together flour, cocoa, soda and salt; set aside. Cream butter, oil, and sugar together. Add eggs and beat well. Mix in zucchini. Add vanilla, nuts and chocolate chips.

Alternately add dry ingredients and buttermilk, mixing after each addition. Pour into greased and floured 9x13-inch pan. Top with extra chocolate chips and nuts.

Bake at 325° for 50 to 60 minutes.

Marilyn Hopson, Lumsden, Canada

sweet ending

Randy's Mandarin Orange Cake

1 cup flour
1 cup sugar
1 egg
1 can mandarin oranges, drained
1 tsp. salt
1 tsp. baking soda
1 tsp. vanilla
1 cup chopped nuts

Frosting:
1/4 cup brown sugar
1 Tb. butter
1 Tb. milk

whipped cream

Combine all ingredients and beat with electric mixer on medium speed until blended. Pour batter into a greased 9-inch square baking pan. Bake at 350° for 30 minutes.

Bring the frosting ingredients to a boil and pour on warm cake. Top with whipped cream.

This is great for a very fast and yummy dessert. Children sometimes call this a chocolate chip cake, but there is no chocolate in this one. Great for school lunches!

Randy Costello, Jacksonville

Oatmeal Cake

Cake:
1-1/4 cups boiling water
1 cup rolled oats
1/2 cup butter
1 cup brown sugar
1 tsp. vanilla
2 eggs
1/4 cup plain yogurt
1-1/4 cups whole wheat pastry flour
1 tsp. baking soda
2 tsp. nutmeg
2 tsp. cloves
2 tsp. cinnamon
1/2 tsp. salt

Topping:
1/4 cup ground almonds
2 Tb. butter
1/4 cup brown sugar
2 Tb. dry milk
1/2 cup coconut

To make cake, pour boiling water over rolled oats and let soak for 20 minutes. Combine remaining cake ingredients. Pour into greased 9-inch pan. Bake at 325° for 55 minutes.

Prepare topping by combining almonds, butter, sugar, milk and coconut together. Spread over hot cake. Broil until bubbly. Watch -- as it only takes a few moments to brown.

Excellent lunch box dessert!

Gingerbread Cake

1/2 cup butter or margarine
1/2 cup brown sugar
2 eggs
1 cup molasses
1 cup water
1 tsp. cinnamon
1 tsp. ginger
1 tsp. cloves
1/2 tsp. salt
1 tsp. baking soda
2-1/2 cups flour
whipped cream or applesauce, optional

Cream butter and brown sugar. Add eggs, one at a time, beating well. Combine water and molasses. Sift together dry ingredients. Alternately add dry ingredients and liquid, beating only until smooth. Bake in well greased and floured 9x13-inch pan for 25-35 minutes at 350°. Cool in pan for 5 minutes.

Serve warm or cold. Top with whipped cream or applesauce.

sweet ending

Trifle

Trifle White Cake:

This plain white cake has a coarse texture that is ideal for drinking up the sherry. Marilyn doesn't use this cake for anything but Trifle.

1/4 pound butter
1 cup sugar
2 eggs
2 cups all-purpose flour

3/4 cup milk
3 tsp. baking powder
1 tsp. vanilla

Cream butter and sugar together. Add eggs, mixing well. Add flour and milk alternately in 3 additions, with the flour last. Add baking powder and vanilla, mixing well. Pour in a greased pan (any size because it will be cut up). Bake at 350° for 30 to 40 minutes. Cool. Cut cake into large pieces and place in bottom of serving bowl (preferably clear). Soak with *1 cup dry sherry.*

28 ounces mixed fruit, fresh or canned (if canned, drain)
3 ounces raspberry jello prepared according to package directions

Mix fruit into almost set gelatin. Add to cake layer. After gelatin is completely set, add custard.

vanilla Custard:

3 Tb. sugar
1-1/2 Tb. cornstarch
3 egg yolks

2-1/2 cups milk
1 tsp. vanilla

Whisk sugar, cornstarch and egg yolks together in a saucepan. Whisk in milk in a thin steady stream. Cook, stirring constantly over medium heat until thickened to a consistency of a custard. Remove from heat and add vanilla, let cool completely.

Top with *whipped cream* and refrigerate for 1 hour or more before serving. May be kept refrigerated for up to 3 days.

Marilyn Goldsmith, Lumsden,Canada

sweet ending

257

Apple Torte Rowena

1 recipe Basic Pie Crust, page 292

Filling:
2 8 ounce packages cream cheese
1/2 cup sugar
2 eggs, lightly beated
1 tsp. vanilla extract

Topping:
3 medium apples, peeled and sliced
1/4 cup sugar
1/2 tsp. cinnamon
1/4 tsp. vanilla extract
1/4 cup coarsely chopped walnuts

Prepare crust according to directions. Roll out or press into a 10-inch springform pan.

Prepare filling: In a large mixing bowl, combine cream cheese, sugar, eggs and vanilla. Mix until well blended and pour into crust.

Prepare topping: Combine sliced apples, sugar, cinnamon and vanilla in a large bowl. Stir to mix well. Layer apple slices on top of cheese mixture, then sprinkle with chopped walnuts.

Bake for 15 minutes at 450°. Reduce heat to 350° and bake an additional 45 minutes. Cool to room temperature. Chill before serving.

The graceful loops and curves of the Old Scenic Highway are easily viewed from the Meyer State Park Overlook, near the entrance to the Governor Tom McCall Preserve at Rowena Plateau. The overlook with its circular drive provides an opportunity to view and photograph panoramic views of the Columbia River Gorge.

258

Gloria's Cheesecake

Crust:
1-1/2 cups graham cracker crumbs
1/3 cup melted butter

Bottom layer:
4 8 ounce packages cream cheese
1 cup sugar
1 tsp. vanilla
1 tsp. almond extract
2 eggs

Topping:
2 cups sour cream
1 tsp. almond extract
3/4 cup sugar
juice of 1/2 lemon

Combine cracker crumbs and butter and pat into bottom of greased 10-inch springform pan. Set aside.

Beat together cream cheese, sugar, vanilla and almond extract. Add eggs, beat until blended. Pour onto crust and bake at 350° on the top shelf of oven for 1/2 hour or until set. Take out and let set for 5 minutes.

Meanwhile, combine topping ingredients. Pour onto top of cheesecake that has set. Bake again for 10 minutes.

Refrigerate all day or overnight.

Gloria Mathews, Bend

Legendary Cheesecake Toppings

Listed here are some favorite toppings. Which one complements your meal best we leave for you to decide.

These toppings are suggested for use with Gloria's Cheesecake, page 259, or with any basic cheesecake recipe. The right topping can bring a whole new dimension to this popular and easy dessert.

whipped cream flavored with your favorite liqueur

sour cream with grated chocolate curls

drizzled-on melted semi-sweet chocolate

strawberry halves, raspberries, or blueberries, glazed with melted currant jelly

thinly sliced kiwi, glazed with melted apricot preserves

lemon curd

honey

s
w
e
e
t

e
n
d
i
n
g

Bridge of the Gods spans the Columbia River from Cascade Locks to Stevenson, Washington. The bridge was built in 1926 and named after the natural bridge of Indian legend. It is located close to Marine Park and Cascade Locks Historical Museum, the latter a storehouse of information about sternwheelers, fishwheels and the building of dams and locks on the Columbia.

Pumpkin Chiffon Cheesecake

serves 12 to 16

Crust:
1 cup graham cracker crumbs
1/2 cup finely chopped nuts *
3 Tb. sugar
3 Tb. melted butter

Filling:
2 8 ounce packages cream cheese
3/4 cup sugar
4 eggs, separated
1 cup canned pumpkin
3 Tb. flour
1 cup half-and-half
1 tsp. vanilla
1-1/2 tsp. cinnamon
1/2 tsp. ginger
1/2 tsp. nutmeg
1/4 tsp. salt

Topping:
1 cup sour cream
2 Tb. sugar
1/2 tsp. vanilla

sweet ending

For the crust, mix together the crumbs, nuts, sugar and melted butter. Press into the bottom and up the sides of a 9-inch springform pan. Bake at 325° for 5 minutes. Set aside.

Whip the cream cheese until light and fluffy. Add the sugar and continue beating, adding egg yolks one at a time. Add pumpkin, flour and half-and- half and beat . Blend in the vanilla, spices and salt. In a separate bowl, beat egg whites until stiff. Fold into the pumpkin mixture. Pour into crust and bake at 325° for 1 hour.

To prepare topping, combine the sour cream, vanilla and sugar and spread over cheesecake. Garnish with pecan halves if desired. Bake 5 minutes more. Chill thoroughly. Enjoy!

* Pecans are Jennifer's favorite.

Jennifer Price, Parkdale

261

Pumpkin Cheesecake

1/2 cup butter
1/3 cup sugar
1 egg
1-1/4 cups flour

1 8 ounce package cream cheese
3/4 cup sugar
1 16 ounce can pumpkin
1 tsp. cinnamon
1/4 tsp. ginger
1/4 tsp. nutmeg
dash salt
2 eggs
whipping cream

Cream butter and sugar until light and fluffy. Blend in egg.
Add flour; mix well. Press dough on bottom and 2 inches up
the side of a 9-inch springform pan. Bake at 400° for
5 minutes. Remove from oven and reduce heat to 350°.

Combine softened cream cheese and sugar until well
blended. Add pumpkin, spices and salt; mix well. Add eggs,
one at a time, mixing well after each addition. Pour mixture
into pastry lined pan. Smooth surface to edge of crust.
Bake at 350° for 50 minutes. Loosen cake from rim of pan;
cool before removing rim. Chill. Garnish with whipped
cream. Serve.

Laura L. Young, Hood River

sweet ending

262

Luscious Baked
Chocolate Cheesecake

1/3 cup butter, melted
1-1/4 cups graham cracker crumbs
1/4 cup sugar
3 8 ounce packages cream cheese, softened
1 14 ounce can sweetened condensed milk
1 12 ounce package semi-sweet chocolate
  chips, melted
4 eggs
2 tsp. vanilla

Combine butter, crumbs and sugar. Pat firmly on bottom of 9-inch springform pan.

In a large mixing bowl, beat cream cheese until fluffy. Add sweetened condensed milk and beat until smooth. Add remaining ingredients and mix well. Pour into prepared pan.

Bake 1 hour at 300° or until cake springs back when lightly touched. Cool to room temperature. Chill.

Remove sides of pan. Garnish as desired.

Joella Dethman, Pine Grove

Summit Silk Pie

Crust:
1-1/2 cups crushed chocolate wafer crumbs
1/4 cup butter, melted
1/3 cup filberts or pecans

Grind the cookies and nuts together in a food processor or blender until fine. Mix butter into the crumbs and press into the bottom of a springform pan. Bake the crust in a 300° oven for about 5 minutes. Cool.

Filling:
18 ounces semi-sweet chocolate pieces
1-1/2 cups sugar
1 cup butter
8 eggs, separate, beat whites separately
1/4 cup cream or half-and-half
1 Tb. vanilla *
whipping cream

Melt the chocolate in a double boiler. Meanwhile, in mixer, cream butter and gradually add sugar. Add eggs one at a time until all are incorporated. Add vanilla or other flavoring.

Add the melted chocolate to the butter mixture and mix well. Add cream slowly and continue to mix.

Pour the chocolate mixture in the pie shell. Refrigerate until set. To serve, garnish with whipped cream and grated chocolate.

* May use liqueur of your choice - Grand Marnier, Frangelico, Raspberry, etc., as a substitute.

sweet ending

Summit is at the east end of Government Camp and was one of the earliest developed ski areas on Mt. Hood.

264

Mousse au Chocolat

serves 5 to 6

4 squares semi-sweet chocolate
rum, kirsch or strong coffee
4 extra large eggs, separated, at room
*   temperature*
1/2 cup fine sugar

Melt chocolate in a little rum, either in microwave or on top of stove. In a separate bowl, beat egg whites until quite stiff. Set aside.

Beat egg yolks in a large bowl, add sugar very gradually until it coats the spoon, about 2 to 3 minutes.

Add melted chocolate and beat to blend. Fold stiff egg whites carefully into chocolate mixture with rubber spatula.

Fill individual custard cups or glasses with mousse. Chill in refrigerator, covered with plastic wrap.

It keeps nicely when refrigerated for 1 to 2 days, or longer, but chances are it will be eaten first!

Mimi Macht, Hood River

sweet ending

Chocolate Torte

Cake:
1-3/4 cups flour
2 cups sugar
3/4 cup cocoa
2 tsp. soda
1 tsp. baking powder
1/2 tsp. salt
2 eggs
1 cup strong coffee
1 cup buttermilk
1/2 cup oil
1 tsp. vanilla

Filling:
1 cup raspberry jam
4 Tb. brandy

Frosting:
8 ounces semi-sweet chocolate chips
2 Tb. solid vegetable shortening

Mix first 6 ingredients together. In separate bowl mix together eggs, coffee, buttermilk, oil and vanilla. Add to dry ingredients and beat on medium speed for 5 minutes. Pour into 2 buttered and floured 9-inch cake pans.

Bake at 350° for 25 to 30 minutes. Cool completely. Remove from pan (you may freeze cake for up to 1 week at this point). Cut each cake in half horizontally to make 2 layers.

Combine jam and brandy and spread on 3 of the 4 slices of cake. Stack layers ending with the one plain layer on top.

Make frosting by melting chocolate and shortening in top of double boiler over simmering water. Pour frosting onto center of cake and spread to flow over entire cake. Chill at least 30 minutes. Even better 2 or 3 days later, but we bet the cake won't be around that long.

You may also make this into two, double layer cakes, or one 9x13-inch cake.

Double Chocolate
Raspberry Tart

serves 10

Cookie crust:
1/2 cup butter, softened
1 Tb. sugar
1 egg yolk
1 cup flour
1/4 tsp. salt
1/2 tsp. vanilla

Mix ingredients together and press in the bottom and 1-inch up the sides of a 9-inch tart pan or pie plate. Bake at 350° for about 11 minutes or until lightly browned. Cool completely.

Filling:
10 ounce package frozen raspberries, thawed
1 Tb. cornstarch
1 Tb. sugar
1 cup fresh raspberries (optional)

1/2 cup butter, softened
1/3 cup sugar
4 ounces white chocolate, chips or squares, melted
2 eggs
2 ounces chocolate, chips or squares
2 Tb. butter

Purée thawed raspberries in blender or food processor; strain and discard seeds. In a small saucepan, combine cornstarch and 1 Tb. sugar, blending well. Gradually add raspberry purée. Cook over low heat until thickened, stirring constantly. Cool and spread over crust. Arrange fresh raspberries over raspberry purée layer. Refrigerate.

In a small bowl, beat 1/2 cup butter and 1/3 cup sugar until light and fluffy. Gradually add melted white chocolate, beating constantly. Add eggs, one at a time, beating on high speed for 3 minutes after each addition. Spread white chocolate mixture over raspberries and refrigerate until set.

In a double boiler or in the microwave, melt dark chocolate together with butter; carefully pour and spread dark chocolate over white chocolate layer. Refrigerate until set. Let stand at room temperature for 30 minutes before serving.

This tart is very impressive in taste as well as looks, definitely worth the extra work for a special occasion!

sweet ending

Chocolate Fudge Torte

Torte:
3/4 cup butter
6 Tb. cocoa
1 cup sugar, divided
2/3 cup ground blanched almonds
2 Tb. flour
3 eggs, separated
2 Tb. water

Melt butter in medium saucepan. Stir in cocoa and 3/4 cup sugar. Blend until smooth. Remove from heat and cool 5 minutes. Blend in almonds and flour. Beat in egg yolks one at a time. Stir in water.

In medium bowl, beat egg whites until foamy. Gradually add remaining 1/4 cup sugar. Beat until soft peaks form. Gently fold chocolate mixture into egg whites, blending thoroughly. Pour into greased and floured 9-inch layer pan.

Bake at 350° for 30 minutes or until toothpick comes out clean. Cool 10 minutes. Cake will settle slightly. Remove from pan. Cool on wire rack.

Glaze:
2 Tb. butter
2 Tb. cocoa
2 Tb. water
1/2 tsp. vanilla
1 cup powdered sugar

Garnish:
raspberries
fresh mint leaves

To make glaze, melt butter in small sauce pan over low heat. Add cocoa and water. Stir constantly until mixture thickens. Do not boil. Remove from heat and add vanilla. Gradually add sugar, beating with a whisk until smooth.

Spread tops and sides with glaze. Garnish with raspberries and mint leaves.

Robin Laurance, Parkdale

Vista Ridge Almond
Fudge Torte

1 tsp. instant coffee powder
2 Tb. hot water
4 ounces semi-sweet chocolate, melted
3 eggs, separated
1/2 cup butter
3/4 cup sugar
1/3 cup almond paste, crumbled
1/2 cup flour

Glaze:
8 ounces semi-sweet chocolate
1 Tb. solid shortening

Dissolve the coffee in the hot water. Stir in the melted chocolate. Beat egg whites just until stiff peaks form.

In another bowl, cream the butter and sugar together. Add the almond paste and beat. Mix in the egg yolks, chocolate mixture and flour. Fold in the egg whites, about 1/3 at a time, just until blended. Spread into a greased and cocoa-dusted 8-inch round cake pan and bake at 350° for 30 minutes. Do not overbake.

Let cool on rack for 10 minutes, then turn out of pan. Cool thoroughly.

Melt together in a double boiler or in a microwave the glaze ingredients. Cool, stirring occasionally, until it thickens slightly. Spread glaze over top and side of torte. Chill. Let warm to room temperature before serving.

Mimi Macht, Hood River

Chocolate Bread Pudding

serves 8 to 10

5 cups milk
2 Tb. butter
1 cup sugar
6 Tb. unsweetened cocoa (preferably Dutch
*   process)*
salt
3/4 loaf sliced French bread, cubed
2 eggs, slightly beaten
2 tsp. vanilla

Heat milk and butter in a large saucepan. Combine sugar and cocoa and add to milk. Salt to taste. Add bread cubes. Cook and stir for 10 minutes. Cool slightly and stir in eggs and vanilla.

Pour into a buttered 8x11-inch baking dish. Bake at 350° for 20 minutes or until a nice "crust" forms and toothpick comes out fairly clean. Cut and serve with a dollop of topping.

Topping:
1/4 cup butter
1 cup sugar
2 eggs
1/2 pint whipping cream

Cut butter into sugar. Beat in eggs. Add whipping cream and beat until fluffy.

Monsignor John A. Lunney, Anchorage, Alaska
In memory of his mother.

s
w
e
e
t

e
n
d
i
n
g

271

Lemon Feather Soufflé

1 Tb. butter
3/4 cup sugar
2 egg yolks
juice and grated rind of one lemon
3 Tb. sifted flour
1 cup milk
2 egg whites, whipped until stiff peaks form

whipped cream, for garnish

Cream butter, sugar and egg yolks. Add lemon juice, rind and flour. Stir well; add milk. Fold in egg whites. Gently pour into lightly buttered soufflé dish. Bake in a pan of water at 325° for about 25 to 30 minutes. Cool.

Serve with a dollop of whipped cream.

Light, refreshing dessert after a heavy meal!

Dorothy Laurance, Parkdale

sweet ending

272

Strawberry Almond Tart

Basic Pie Crust, page 292
raw rice or pie weights for weighting the shell
1 cup blanched almonds
2/3 cup sugar
2 large eggs, beaten lightly
1/4 tsp. almond extract
2 pints strawberries, hulled and halved
*   lenghtwise*
3/4 cup strawberry, currant or raspberry jelly

Roll dough 1/8-inch thick and fit into 2 medium- size tart pans (any shape will work). Fold over top edge and crimp as desired. Prick the bottom of the shells lightly with a fork and chill for 30 minutes.

Line shells with wax paper and fill with rice or weights. Place the pans on a cookie sheet and bake the shells for 12 minutes at 425°. Remove wax paper and rice and bake for about 5 minutes. Remove from oven and cool.

In a food processor or blender, grind the almonds with the sugar until it forms a powder. Add eggs and almond extract. Blend until combined well. Spoon the almond paste carefully over the bottom of each cooled crust.

Bake the shells for 20 minutes at 350° or until the almond paste is golden.

Cool completely. Remove the shells from the tart pans and place on serving platter.

Arrange strawberries decoratively over the top of tarts. Brush with melted warm jelly.

Let cool completely and serve.

s
w
e
e
t

e
n
d
i
n
g

Fresh Blueberry Bark

1 cup fresh blueberries*
12 ounces highest quality white chocolate

Wash and pat dry blueberries. Melt white chocolate in microwave. Gently stir fresh blueberries into chocolate. Pour chocolate and blueberries on to a sheet of waxed paper. Let mixture harden at room temperature.

Break into serving pieces and serve on a red plate.

*Only fresh blueberries can be used

This is attractive and timely for the 4th of July!

Sandra Haynie, Hood River

Raspberry Flan

1 cup flour
dash of salt
2 Tb. sugar
1/2 cup butter
1 Tb. vinegar

1 cup sugar
2 Tb. flour
3 cups raspberries*
powdered sugar

Combine flour, salt, and sugar. Add butter and vinegar and mix well with hands. Press gently into a 9-inch pie plate.

Mix together gently; sugar, flour, and 2 cups raspberries. Place on crust in pie plate. Bake at 400° for 50 to 60 minutes. Sprinkle with powdered sugar and remaining 1 cup raspberries after removing from oven.

*Try other fesh fruits and berries, such as peaches or blueberries.

sweet ending

Peach Melba

2 cups fresh or frozen raspberries
2 Tb. cornstarch
3/4 cup sugar
1 Tb. butter
dash cinnamon
2 Tb. Cointreau
2 fresh peaches
vanilla ice cream

Thaw berries and mix in a saucepan with cornstarch. Cook on medium heat until it thickens. Add sugar and cook about 2 minutes. Remove from heat. Stir in butter, cinnamon and Cointreau. Set aside to cool.

Dip peaches in boiling water for a few seconds to loosen skin. Peel and cut in half. Remove pit and put each peach half in a small dish or champagne glass. Put a scoop of ice cream in each half and spoon warm sauce over the top. Serve immediately.

Sauce can be made ahead of time and warmed over, but do not boil.

Tom Temple, Bend

sweet ending

Hood River Brandied Cherries

6 pounds Hood River Lambert cherries*
1-1/2 cups sugar
1-1/3 cups water
2 Tb. lemon juice
1-1/2 cups Hood River Monarch Brandy

Wash, stem and pit cherries. Prepare by sterilizing 6 pint jars and
lids for boiling water bath.

Combine sugar, water and lemon juice in a saucepan. Boil to
dissolve sugar.

In hot jars, pour 1/4 cup hot syrup over cherries that are tightly
packed to within 1/2 inch of top, add 1/4 cup brandy and more syrup
if necessary to cover cherries.

Shake, releasing air bubbles, wipe jar rim, and close jar tightly with
lid. Process in boiling water bath for 20 minutes.**

Ways to use cherries:

Pour cherries and syrup directly over vanilla ice cream. Easy and
wonderful.

Drain cherries and add 2 tsp. cornstarch to reserved syrup. Stir,
bring to a boil until thickened. Reheat cherries in sauce and serve.

To flame: pour warm cherries and syrup in shallow skillet or chafing
dish. Pour 2 Tb. of warmed brandy on cherries. Light with match.
Stir until flame is gone and spoon over cake or ice cream.

*Any dark sweet variety of cherries will work.

** Please follow manufacturers instructions for safe canning
techniques.

Sydney Blaine, Parkdale

sweet ending

Rhubarb Cream Pastry

serves 8

Cookie crust:
1/3 cup butter, softened
1 Tb. sugar
1 egg yolk
1 cup flour
1 tsp. vanilla
dash of salt

Filling:
3 cups sliced fresh rhubarb
2 Tb. butter
4 Tb. flour
1 cup sugar
2 eggs
1 cup heavy cream

Mix all cookie crust ingredients together and pat into a 9-inch tart pan or any other 9- inch round pan. Spread rhubarb over the crust. Combine and mix remaining ingredients and pour over the rhubarb. Bake at 350° for 50 minutes or until set.

Serve with vanilla ice cream or whipped cream.

Anne's Butter Tarts

makes 4 dozen small tarts

48 small tart shells

2 eggs
1 cup brown sugar
1/4 cup corn syrup
1/4 cup butter
2 tsp. vinegar
1 tsp. vanilla
1 cup currants or raisins
1/4 tsp. salt

Beat all together until full of bubbles. Fill tart shells and bake at 400° for approximately 20 minutes.

Anne Holman, Lumsden, Canada

Washington Fresh
Blueberry Tart

serves 6

Shortbread crust:
1 cup flour
2 Tb. powdered sugar
1/2 cup butter

Combine flour and sugar. Cut in butter until mixture resembles cornmeal. Chill for 30 minutes. Turn into a 9-inch tart or pie pan. Press firmly onto bottom and sides of pan. Bake at 425° for 10 minutes or until golden. Cool.

Filling:
2 cups fresh blueberries
1 jar (10 ounces) or 1 cup red currant jelly
1 cup sour cream
2 Tb. walnuts, finely chopped and toasted

Rinse blueberries, drain and dry well. Spread on cooled crust. Melt jelly over low heat. Cool slightly, then spread evenly over blueberries. Spread with sour cream, without touching crust, and sprinkle with walnuts.

Bev Elsner, Husum

s
w
e
e
t

e
n
d
i
n
g

Pear Tart

1 cup flour
5 Tb. butter
6 Tb. sugar, divided
1/3 cup water, divided
6 Bosc pears, or other firm ripe pears
1 10 ounce jar apricot preserves
1 tsp. lemon juice

Prepare pastry by mixing flour, butter, 2 Tb. sugar and
2 Tb. cold water together. Butter a 9-inch tart pan and press
pastry into pan and up sides. Chill.

Peel and core 3 pears, cut into chunks and blend at high
speed in a food processor or blender with 1/4 cup water,
2 Tb. sugar and 1/3 cup preserves. Simmer in saucepan until
thick.

Peel and slice into 1/8-inch wedges the 3 remaining pears.
Toss with 2 Tb. sugar and lemon juice.

Spread sauce over pastry and arrange slices overlapping in a
circular manner. Bake at 400° for 45 minutes, until tender and
brown.

Heat remaining preserves until boiling, brush over tart evenly.
Cool on wire rack. To serve, remove sides of pan and slice.

Charlene Rivers, Parkdale

Fresh Fruit Pizza

serves 2

1/4 cup butter
1/4 cup brown sugar
1 tsp. cinnamon
4 apples, plums or peaches*

4 eggs, separated
1/3 cup sugar
1/3 cup flour
1/2 tsp. baking powder
1/3 cup milk

In a 400° oven melt butter in a 10-inch round baking dish.
Remove from oven and sprinkle with brown sugar and
cinnamon. Slice fruit and arrange in dish. Bake for 8 to
10 minutes.

Meanwhile, beat egg whites until foamy and gradually beat in
sugar until stiff. In another bowl, combine flour and baking
powder, beat in milk and yolks, then fold in egg white mixture.
Spread evenly over fruit. Bake 20 minutes. Invert onto
serving platter.

*Excellent anytime of the year as you may use either fresh or
  frozen fruit.

s
w
e
e
t

e
n
d
i
n
g

281

Sharon's Fruit Pizza

Crust:
2 cups flour
1/2 cup brown sugar
1/4 cup powdered sugar
1 cup butter

Topping:
12 ounces cream cheese
1/2 cup sugar
1 tsp. vanilla
fruit in season*

Glaze:
1/2 cup orange juice
1/2 cup sugar
1/2 cup water
2 Tb. cornstarch
dash of salt

Mix ingredients together for the crust. Press into 2 pizza
pans. Bake at 350° for 8 to 12 minutes. Cool.

Beat together cream cheese, 1/2 cup sugar and vanilla.
Spread on crust. Arrange fruit in circular pattern. You may use
any fruit combination (*blueberries, raspberries or sliced
stawberries, nectarines, bananas, kiwi, pear, apple).

Cook the orange juice, sugar, water, cornstarch and salt until
thick and bubbly, to make a glaze. Once cool, brush this over
the fruit.

Use your food processor for a quick and easy method of
preparing both crust and topping.

Enjoy! Beautiful and great for any season.

Sharon Fitzsimmons, Lumsden, Canada

Cheese & Pear Pizza

2 D'Anjou pears
Fruit Fresh
1 sheet puff pastry, thawed*
15 ounces ricotta cheese
3 ounces cream cheese
1/2 cup powdered sugar
1 tsp. grated lemon peel
1/4 cup toasted, sliced or chopped pecans

Peel 2 D'Anjou pears; core and slice in 1/8- inch slices. Toss slices lightly in Fruit Fresh to coat so they don't turn brown. Set aside.

Bake the puff pastry at 450° for 10 minutes on an ungreased cookie sheet. Cool.

Beat ricotta cheese, cream cheese, powdered sugar and the lemon peel together, and spread on cooled, baked pastry. Arrange pear slices over cheese. Sprinkle toasted pecans over pears.

Note: To toast pecans, spread on baking pan and bake for 3 to 5 minutes at 350°. Stir once during that time. Chop after toasting.

*Find puff pastry in the freezer section of most supermarkets.

Myrtle White, Hood River

Summer Fruit Pie

Crust:
1-1/2 cups flour
1/4 tsp. salt
1/2 cup butter
1 egg yolk
2 Tb. milk

Filling:
1 Tb. glaze
8 ounces cream cheese
1-1/2 cups strawberries
2 or 3 peaches

Glaze:
1/2 cup apricot or peach preserves
2 to 3 tsp. water
1/8 tsp. almond extract

Prepare crust and bake at 425° for 15 minutes. Cool.

Make a glaze by combining preserves, water and almond extract. Combine 1 Tb. glaze with cream cheese. Spread on cooled pie crust. Top with strawberries and peaches. Pour or brush glaze on fruit. Chill before serving.

Open Face Pear Pie

1 9- inch unbaked pie shell
1/4 cup butter
1 cup sugar
3 eggs
1/4 cup flour
1 tsp. vanilla
1/8 tsp. salt
4 medium ripe D'Anjou or Bartlett pears, peeled,
    cored and halved (or 8 canned pear halves)
mace

Cream sugar, butter and eggs. Add remaining ingredients
and beat well. Arrange pears on unbaked pie shell with
points toward center, and one in the center. Pour the egg
mixture over pears and sprinkle with mace. Bake for
approximately 45 minutes in a 350° oven until custard is
golden and set.

Mary Moore, Hood River

Sour Cream Pear Pie

1 9-inch pastry shell
1 cup sour cream
1 egg
3/4 cup sugar
1 tsp. vanilla
1/4 tsp. salt
2 Tb. flour
4 cups peeled, diced ripe Bartlett pears
   (or pears of your choice)

Blend the sour cream, egg, sugar, vanilla, salt and flour until smooth. Fold in the prepared pears. Pour into the pie shell. Bake at 375° for 40 minutes. Sprinkle with Pecan Streusel Topping and bake another 10 minutes. Cool slightly and serve.

Pecan Streusel Topping:
1/4 cup flour
1/4 cup brown sugar
1 tsp. cinnamon
1/4 cup butter, cut in small pieces
1/4 cup finely chopped pecans

Cut butter into combined flour, sugar and cinnamon. Add pecans.

Nona Moore, Parkdale
Mary Moore, Hood River

sweet ending

286

Lillian's Pear Pie

2 eggs
2 tsp. vanilla
1-1/2 cups sugar
1/2 cup flour
2 tsp. baking powder
2 cups chopped pears (about 2 large)
1/4 tsp. salt
1 cup chopped walnuts or pecans

Beat eggs, add vanilla and sugar. Add flour, baking powder and salt. Stir to combine. Fold in pears. Turn into a well-greased 11-inch pie plate. Sprinkle with chopped nuts. Bake at 350° for 35 minutes.

This pie puffs up during baking and as it cools it falls.

Lillian Foster, Hood River

Known throughout the world for its moderate climate, rich soils, and favorable growing seasons, Oregon's Hood River Valley is ideally suited to the production of the finest pears and apples.

sweet ending

Bartlett Praline Pie

serves 8

5 to 7 fresh ripe Bartlett pears, cored and sliced
2/3 cup sugar
1/4 cup flour
1/2 tsp. grated lemon peel
1/2 tsp. ground ginger
dash of salt

1 9-inch unbaked pastry shell, page 292
whipping cream

Toss pears with sugar, flour, lemon peel, ginger and salt.
Place about 1/3 cup praline mixture in the bottom of the pie
shell. Add the pears. Sprinkle with the remaining topping.
Bake at 400° for 35 minutes. Serve warm with whipped cream.

Praline Topping:
1/2 cup firmly packed brown sugar
1/3 cup flour
1/4 cup butter
2/3 cup chopped pecans

Combine brown sugar and flour. Cut in butter until crumbly
and add pecans.

Strawberry-Rhubarb
Cream Pie

1-1/2 cup shortening
3 cups flour
3/4 cup water

4 cups chopped rhubarb
1/2 cup strawberries
3 eggs, beaten
1-1/2 cups sugar
2 Tb. butter
1/4 cup flour
3/4 tsp. nutmeg

Blend the shortening into the flour. Add the water and mix.
Press into 2 round balls, flattened on the top. Roll out the
bottom crust on a floured pastry cloth.

Fit into a 10-inch pie pan. In a large bowl mix the fruit and
eggs. Combine the dry ingredients and add to the fruit
mixture. Stir. Pour into the pastry shell. Top with 2 Tb.
butter. Roll out and add the top crust.

Slash top decoratively for steam to escape. Bake at 400° for
1 hour. Cool.

Enjoy with a scoop of vanilla ice cream.

*Recipe offered by The Flying L Ranch, compliments of
Judith Lloyd.*

Oregon Apple Pie

Pastry:
2 cups unsifted all-purpose flour
1 Tb. sugar
1 tsp. salt
2/3 cup plus 2 Tb. shortening
2 to 4 Tb. cold water

Filling:
3/4 cup sugar
1 Tb. flour
1 Tb. cornstarch
1/2 tsp. ground cinnamon

pinch of nutmeg
5 to 6 Gravenstein
  apples
2 Tb. butter
1 Tb. sugar

Prepare pastry: In medium-size bowl, combine flour, sugar, and salt. With pastry blender or 2 knives, cut in shortening until mixture resembles coarse crumbs. Stir in water, 1 Tb. at a time, until pastry holds together. Set aside.

Prepare filling: In large bowl, combine 3/4 cup sugar, flour, cornstarch, cinnamon, and nutmeg. Peel, core, and slice apples 1/4- inch thick. Toss apple slices in sugar mixture until well coated.

Divide pastry into 2 portions, one slightly larger than the other. On lightly floured board, roll larger piece to an 11- inch circle. Fit into 9-inch pie plate. Spoon filling into crust; dot with butter. Roll out remaining dough to a 10- inch circle and place over apple mixture. Moisten edges of pastry; press together, turn edges under, and flute. Cut a slit in top crust. Sprinkle with sugar, if desired.

Bake at 425° for 45 to 50 minutes, or until crust is golden brown and apples are tender. Cool on wire rack.

Compliments of Ruth Honeyman of Scholls Ferry Farm, Beaverton.

Scholls Ferry Farm uses its own apples as well as Hood River Valley fruits for its commercial butters, cider jelly, chutney, and fresh squeezed cider.

s
w
e
e
t

e
n
d
i
n
g

290

Buttermilk Pie

1/4 cup flour
2 cups sugar
1/2 cup butter, melted
3 eggs
1 tsp. vanilla
3/4 cup buttermilk
1/4 tsp. nutmeg
9-inch pie crust, unbaked (see page 292)

Blend ingredients and place in unbaked pie crust. Bake at
350° for about 40 to 45 minutes.

A wonderful old-fashioned pie with incredible flavor!

Jan Tatyrek, Odell

Basic Pie Crust

Makes one double 9-inch pie crust

2-1/2 cups flour
1/4 tsp. salt
1 tsp. sugar (optional)
1 cup butter, cut in small pieces
1/4 to 1/2 cup ice water

Put flour, salt and sugar in food processor.

Add butter and process 10 seconds. Add enough ice water, one Tb. at a time, and process until dough holds together without crumbling, no longer than 30 seconds.

Press each ball into a flat circle. Wrap in plastic and chill for one hour.

When ready to use, roll each circle out on lightly floured board to 1/8-inch thickness.

For partially baked pastry, prick the bottom of the crust and line pastry with aluminum foil; weight with beans. Bake at 375° for 10 to12 minutes. For completely baked, 15 to18 minutes.

Unbaked pastry shells may be refrigerated for up to one day, wrapped well in plastic.

sweet ending

Bessie's Apple Dumplings

serves 8

2 cups flour
2 Tb. sugar
1/2 tsp. salt
4 tsp. baking powder

4 Tb. shortening
3/4 cup milk

4 medium apples, peeled, cored and cut in half
8 tsp. sugar
cinnamon or nutmeg
lemon juice

Mix together the first 4 ingredients. Cut in shortening. Add milk gradually to dry ingredients to make a soft dough. Separate dough into 8 equal pieces, then roll each piece into a circle large enough to hold the apple. Place 1 apple half in center of each (cored side up) and put 1 tsp. sugar into the apple. Add cinnamon or nutmeg and sprinkle with lemon juice. Place a pat of butter on top. Moisten edge of pastry with water; bring opposite edges to center and press together leaving a small opening for steam to escape.

Bake at 425° for 10 minutes. Reduce to 350° and bake for 15 to 20 minutes longer. Serve warm with Brandy Sauce, or vanilla ice cream.

Brandy Sauce:

1/2 cup sugar   nutmeg
1-1/2 Tb. cornstarch   2 cups warm water
1 egg   1 Tb. butter
pinch of salt   1 Tb. vanilla or brandy

Mix first 5 ingredients together well; add water gradually and bring to a boil over medium heat. Stir and cook until it thickens (adjust thickness by adding water if needed). Add the butter and brandy or flavoring of your choice. Spoon sauce over warm baked apples.

This recipe is from a very special friend.

Bessie Huck, Parkdale

Grandpa's Plum Dumplings

makes 20 dumplings

1 package dry yeast
1 tsp. sugar
1/4 cup warm water

3 cups flour
1 tsp. salt
1 egg
2 Tb. butter, melted
1 cup warm milk

20 fresh Italian prunes*

melted butter
cinnamon/sugar mixture

Mix the yeast, sugar and water together. Let proof.

Mix together the flour, salt, egg, butter and warm milk. Add to the yeast mixture and knead this soft dough for 5 to 7 minutes. Place in greased bowl and cover. Let rise for one hour.

Punch down and press into a large rectangle with your hands. Cut into 20 pieces about 3-inches square. Place one prune in center of each square and press opposite edges together to close.

Drop 3 to 4 dumplings at a time into boiling water in very large kettle and cook for about 7 minutes. Test dumpling to see if dough is done.

To serve, pour melted butter over dumplings and sprinkle with cinnamon/sugar mixture.

*You may also use fresh cherries, three per dumpling.

A fruit dumpling traditionally served as the main course in the Old Country.

Take the scenic route through the beautiful Hood River Valley, and see it as you have never seen it before.

Several daily excursions depart from the Hood River Depot in the heart of the Columbia River Gorge. The route winds along the banks of the cascading Hood River, switching back through tall timber to climb the steep walls of the river canyon. Spring and fall excursions will make a 17 mile loop through miles of orchard to Odell and return.

Tuesday excursions from May 31 through October 2, and Labor Day will continue through to Parkdale, with some connecting motor coach to Timberline Lodge. Other special excursions will be scheduled throughout the summer.

To make your trip even more relaxing, snacks and beverages are served aboard the "Lewis and Clark Traveller's Rest" lounge.

The Mount Hood Railroad will take you to scenes of the Hood River Valley which you can only see from the rails. Join them for a leisurely ride on the "Fruit Blossom Special".

Chocolate Pear Crisp

4 cups Bartlett pears
2 cups sugar
2 eggs, beaten*
1/2 cup oil
2 tsp. vanilla
juice of 1 lemon
1 Tb. grated lemon peel
2 cups flour
2 tsp. baking soda
1 tsp. salt
2 tsp. cinnamon
1/2 cup nuts, chopped
1 cup chocolate chips

Peel and cut up pears. Mix with sugar and let sit for 20 minutes.

Meanwhile, mix together the eggs, oil, vanilla, lemon juice and lemon peel. In separate bowl blend together the flour, baking soda, salt and cinnamon. Stir in nuts and chocolate. Add to the oil mixture.

Combine mixture with the pear. Spread in a 9x13-inch greased baking dish. Bake until golden brown, about 50 to 60 minutes at 350°. Serve warm with vanilla ice cream or whipped cream or can be served cold.

*May substitute 3 egg whites for whole eggs, if desired.

Kate Mills, Mt. Hood

s
w
e
e
t

e
n
d
i
n
g

Any Berry Cobbler

1/2 cup butter
1-1/2 cup sugar
1 cup flour
3/4 cup milk
2 tsp. baking powder
3 cups berries, any variety, or peaches

Melt butter in 9x13-inch baking dish. Mix 1 cup sugar, flour, baking powder, and milk. Pour over melted butter. Cover top of batter with fruit.

Sprinkle remaining sugar over fruit. Bake at 350° until batter is golden brown, about 30 minutes. Serve hot with whipped cream or ice cream.

Kathy Oates, Hood River

Plum Crisp

s
w
e
e
t

e
n
d
i
n
g

1/2 cup chopped blanched almonds
1 Tb. honey
1/2 cup whole wheat flour
2 Tb. wheat germ
1/4 tsp. salt
1/4 cup butter, diced
2 pounds fresh plums
1 Tb. lemon juice
1 Tb. honey, or to taste
1 cup plain yogurt

In a medium bowl mix the almonds, honey, flour, wheat germ and salt. Add butter and work into the mixture with your fingers until well blended and crumbly. Refrigerate while preparing the fruit.

Arrange the plums cut side up in a baking dish. Combine lemon and honey and sprinkle over plums. Spoon the almond mixture over the fruit and bake at 375° for 30 minutes until it's crisp and light brown. Cool for 15 minutes and serve with a dollop of yogurt.

Fresh Fruit Paradise

8 cups of fruit; *sliced apples, pears, peaches, raspberries, blueberries, plums, blackberries or huckleberries. You may use any combination of fruit, or only one. Peaches and blueberries together are our favorite.*

1-1/2 cups brown sugar
1/2 cup flour
nutmeg, to taste
cinnamon, to taste
2 Tb. lemon juice or kirsch

Combine brown sugar, flour, numeg and cinnamon together in a large bowl. Gently fold in fruit of your choice. Place fruit mixture in a buttered 9x13-inch baking dish and sprinkle with lemon juice or kirsch. Cover with your choice of topping and bake according to directions below.

Crumb topping:
1 cup flour
1 cup oatmeal
3/4 cup brown sugar
cinnamon
nutmeg
cardamon
1/2 cup butter

Combine dry ingredients and cut in butter until well incorporated. Sprinkle over fruit mixture and bake at 350° for 20-30 minutes.

Cream Cheese Pastry Topping:
6 ounces cream cheese
1/2 cup butter
2 Tb. sugar
1-1/2 cups flour

Combine cream cheese, butter, and sugar in a food processor or with a pastry cutter. Blend in flour to form a dough. Pat into a flat circle about 1-inch thick. Refrigerate for 30 minutes or until dough handles nicely. Remove from refrigerator and roll out 1-inch larger than baking dish. Lay on top; crimp edges and slash top. Bake at 350° for 50 minutes. Let cool all day to set up filling.

Peach Pastry

Pastry:
1 cup margarine
2-1/2 cups flour
1 tsp. salt
1 egg yolk plus enough milk to make 2/3 cup liquid

1 cup crushed corn flakes

Filling:
6 to 8 fresh peaches
1/2 cup sugar
1/2 tsp. cinnamon
1 tsp. vanilla

2 Tb. butter
1 egg white, beaten until stiff peaks form

Glaze:
1 cup powdered sugar
2 Tb. milk

Mix the pastry ingredients, blending like pie crust. Roll out half of pastry and place on pizza pan. Sprinkle corn flakes on pastry.

Peel and slice peaches, stir in sugar, cinnamon and vanilla. Pour over pastry. Dot with butter. Roll out second half of pastry and place on top of fruit filling. Seal edges. Spread egg whites over top pastry.

Bake at 375° for 40 minutes or until golden brown. Drizzle with glaze while warm.

Arlene uses pie cherries or apples for this family favorite.

Arlene Allegre, Hood River

sweet ending

Grandma's Apple Squares

2-1/2 cups flour
1 cup solid vegetable shortening
1/2 tsp. salt
2 Tb. sugar
2 egg yolks plus enough milk to make 2/3 cup
sugar
cinnamon
lemon juice
5 Tb. butter
8-10   Golden Delicious apples or a combination
*   of Goldens, Newtowns, or other tart cooking*
*   apples, peeled, cored and thinly sliced*
1/2 cup graham cracker or bread crumbs

Mix together like pie crust, flour, salt and sugar. Cut in
shortening; add egg yolk mixture. Divide in two and roll each
piece to fit a 10x14-inch jelly roll pan.

Lay down the first crust. Sprinkle crust with the bread cumbs.
Lay apples on top and sprinkle with sugar and cinnamon to
taste. Dot with butter and sprinkle with lemon juice. Cover
with remaining dough. Pinch edges together.

Bake at 350° for 40 minutes or until golden brown. Drizzle
with glaze while warm.

Glaze:
2 cups powdered sugar
1/4 cup milk or enough to make a thin frosting

*This recipe came from the kitchen of Rose Arazim, who for
years blessed us with her great cooking and a humor to
match. She made this recipe once for us using hard, green
Gravenstein apples and it still tasted wonderful!*

sweet ending

Caramel Baked Bosc

serves 8

4 ripe Bosc pears
lemon juice
3/4 cup brown sugar
3 Tb. butter
1/2 cup water

vanilla ice cream or whipped cream

Halve and core pears. Brush each with lemon juice. Place in a baking dish cut side up. Combine remaining 3 ingredients in a saucepan. Bring to a boil and cook for 3 minutes. Pour over pears. Cover the dish with foil and bake at 350° for 30 minutes. Uncover and bake for an additional 10 minutes basting with the syrup from the bottom of the dish. Serve warm with ice cream or whipped cream.

s
w
e
e
t

e
n
d
i
n
g

Hood River Baked Apples

6 Red or Golden Delicious apples, cored

Mixture:
6 Tb. light brown sugar
6 Tb. dry bread crumbs
2 Tb. butter
3/4 tsp. cinnamon
1/4 tsp. nutmeg
2 Tb. raisins

1-1/4 cups boiling water
soft whipped cream, ice cream or sauce

Stuff apples with mixture. Pour boiling water around apples that are in a baking dish. Bake covered, at 375° for 50 minutes. Baste often.

Serve with soft whipped cream, ice cream or your favorite hot sweet sauce.

Recipe offered by Hood River Village Resort.

Hood River Village Resort

s
w
e
e
t

e
n
d
i
n
g

Huckleberry Buckle

1/4 cup oil
1/2 cup sugar
1 egg or 2 egg whites
1 cup flour
1-1/2 tsp. baking powder
1/4 tsp. salt
1/3 cup milk
2 cups huckleberries*

Topping:
1/2 cup sugar
1/3 cup flour
1/2 tsp. cinnamon
1/4 cup butter

Cream the oil and sugar together with the egg until light and fluffy. Mix together the flour, baking powder and salt. Stir these two mixtures together alternately with the milk, beating until smooth. Pour batter into an 8x8-inch greased baking pan. Sprinkle berries over the batter.

For a topping, mix together the sugar, flour and cinnamon. Cut in butter until crumbly. Sprinkle topping over berries.

Bake at 375° for 45 minutes or until cake is golden brown. Serve warm either plain or with Lemon Sauce, page 321.

*Blueberries may be substituted.

Eat or give to neighbors!

Recipe donated by Mary Schlick, Mt. Hood.

Apple Oatmeal Chews

1/2 cup melted butter
1 egg
2/3 cup dark brown sugar
1 tsp. grated orange rind
1/4 tsp. vanilla

1 cup flour
1/2 tsp. soda
1/2 tsp. salt
1 tsp. cinnamon
1/8 tsp. allspice

2 cups grated apples
1-1/3 cups oatmeal
powdered sugar

Cream together first 5 ingredients. Combine next 5 dry ingredients and add to creamed mixture. Stir in apples and oatmeal. Pour into a greased 9 x13-inch baking pan. Bake at 350° for 30 minutes. Cool and dust with powdered sugar.

Bette Benjamin, Parkdale

Pumpkin Bars

Bars:
4 eggs
2 cups sugar
2 cups pumpkin
1 tsp. vanilla
1 cup oil
2 tsp. cinnamon
2 cups flour
3/4 tsp. salt
1 tsp. baking soda

Icing:
1   3 ounce package cream cheese
1 cup butter
1 pound powdered sugar
1 tsp. vanilla

Beat together eggs, sugar, pumpkin, vanilla and oil. Blend together the dry ingredients and beat into oil mixture. Pour batter into a greased 18x17-inch baking pan.

Bake at 350° for 30 minutes.

Combine icing ingredients and spead over cooled bar. Cut into 2-inch squares.

Freezes well.

Jannie Tollerud, Odell

Pumpkin Squares

1/2 cup butter
1 cup brown sugar
1 cup flour
1/2 tsp. baking soda
1/2 tsp. baking powder
1 tsp. vanilla
1 tsp. cinnamon
1/4 tsp. ginger
1/4 tsp. nutmeg
2/3 cup pumpkin
2 eggs
1/2 cup chopped nuts

Combine all ingredients except nuts in large bowl and beat 2 minutes at medium speed. Fold in nuts. Spread evenly in a greased 9x13-inch pan. Bake for 20 to 25 minutes at 350°. Cool. You may frost with favorite orange icing, whipped cream or leave plain.

sweet ending

306

Pumpkin Pie Cake

1 cup sugar
3 eggs
1 large can pumpkin
1 large can evaporated milk
4 tsp. pumpkin pie spice mix
1 box yellow cake mix
1 cup coarsely chopped walnuts or pecans
1-1/2 cubes melted butter

whipped cream for garnish

Beat together first 5 ingredients and pour into an ungreased 9x13-inch pan. Sprinkle cake mix evenly over the top. Sprinkle the chopped nuts over the cake mix. Drizzle the melted butter over the entire cake and press the nuts down slightly. Bake at 350° for 50 minutes or until toothpick inserted comes out clean.

Best served warm with whipped cream.

Turtle Cake

serves 10 to 30

1 box German chocolate cake mix
1/2 cup evaporated milk
1 14 ounce package Kraft caramels
3/4 cup butter
1 8 ounce chocolate bar
1 cup chopped pecans

Before beginning cake, break up chocolate bar in small pieces, chop pecans and unwrap caramels. Place caramels, milk and butter in a double boiler over low heat and melt. While caramel mixture is melting, prepare cake.

Mix cake according to package instructions and pour half of batter into a greased 9x13-inch pan. Bake at 350° for 15 minutes.

Remove cake from oven and pour melted caramels over cake. Spread chocolate bar pieces and pecans over top. Pour other half of cake over that and bake for an additional 20 minutes. Do not bake any longer than 20 minutes. Cool.

Small portions are adequate as this is a very rich, chocoholic's fantasy!

Eloise Dunn , Hood River

sweet ending

Cocoa Brownies

1/3 cup plus 1 Tb. shortening
2 squares unsweetened chocolate
1 cup sugar
2 eggs
3/4 cup flour
1/2 tsp. baking powder
1/2 tsp. salt
1/2 cup chopped nuts

Melt shortening and add chocolate. Beat together sugar and egg until well blended. Meanwhile combine dry ingredients. Add warm chocolate mixture to eggs and sugar; beat well. Add dry ingredients just until blended; stir in nuts.

Spread into a greased 8-inch square pan and bake at 350° for 30 minutes. Do not overbake. While brownies are baking make frosting.

Frosting:
2 Tb. shortening
4 Tb. cocoa
1 cup powdered sugar
1/4 tsp. salt
1-1/2 Tb. heavy cream
1/2 tsp. vanilla

Melt shortening and add cocoa. Measure together sugar, salt and cream. Add hot cocoa mixture and vanilla. Beat all ingredients together and spread on brownies while they are warm. Frosting will melt slightly making it easy to spread and will harden when the brownies cool.

Mary Mauroni, Parkdale

Eagle Creek Chocolate Bars

2/3 cup butter
4 Tb. cocoa
1 cup sugar
2 eggs, slightly beaten
3 cups finely crushed graham crackers
1 cup chopped walnuts
1-1/2 cups coconut
2 tsp. vanilla

Blend first 4 ingredients in a double boiler and cook until smooth and thick.

Add next 4 ingredients, mixing well. Press into bottom of a buttered 9x13-inch pan and chill.

Filling:
1 cup butter
2 cups powdered sugar
3 tsp. milk

Beat together well and spread over chilled bottom. Chill, then frost.

Frosting:
1 large chocolate bar or 12 ounces chocolate chips

Melt in a double boiler and spread on top. Chill briefly until frosting sets. Remove from refrigerator about 15 minutes before serving so crust will cut through nicely.

s
w
e
e
t

e
n
d
i
n
g

Eagle Creek Campground offers a variety of sightseeing opportunities. The larger pools are popular for swimming, with picnicking on the shores. Eagle Creek is accessible from I-84, approximately 18 miles west of Hood River.

Pecan Bites

makes 24

Pastry:
4 ounces cream cheese
1/2 cup margarine
1 cup flour

Filling:
1 egg
3/4 cup brown sugar
1 Tb. butter
1 tsp. vanilla
dash salt
2/3 cup pecans, chopped and divided

Blend ingredients for pastry and chill 1 hour or longer. Shape into 24 small balls. Put 1 ball in bottom of each of 24 tiny muffin cups. Press them until pastry lines cups. Set aside.

Beat together egg, sugar and butter. Add vanilla and salt. Put half the nuts in pastry lined cups, then egg mixture and top with rest of nuts.

Bake at 325° for 45 minutes.

Oregon Walnut Clusters

1/4 cup butter
1/2 cup sugar
1 egg
1/2 cup flour
1/4 tsp. baking powder
1/2 tsp. salt
1-1/2 tsp. vanilla
2 cups broken walnuts
1-1/2 squares semi-sweet chocolate, melted

Sift dry ingredients. Cream butter, sugar, egg and vanilla until creamy. Add melted chocolate. Stir in flour mixture and walnuts.

Drop by teaspoon, 1 inch apart on a greased cookie sheet. Bake at 350° for 10 minutes. Recipe can be doubled. Enjoy!

Aileen Pobanz, Hood River

sweet ending

312

Wy'East Naturals

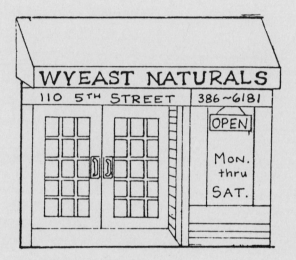

 Open 6 days a week to offer you the best choices in organic products. Grains, seeds, spices, and pastas, many in bulk, as well as fresh ground peanut butter, local produce and dairy products can be found in this friendly market.

Wy'East Naturals has a special daily soup and a selection of fresh garden or pasta salads, burritos and sandwiches.

When summer is here to stay, drop in and "pick your picnic" for a power lunch to take with you for an excursion on The Mt. Hood Railroad.

313

Wy'East Naturals Chocolate Chip Cookies

makes 30 large cookies

1 pound butter
6 cups brown sugar
6 large eggs
3 tsp. vanilla
1-1/2 cups water

3/4 tsp. salt
1-1/2 tsp. baking powder
1-1/2 tsp. baking soda
8 cups whole wheat pastry flour
4-1/2 cups coconut, macaroon
2-1/4 cups wheat germ
4 cups chocolate chips
3-1/2 cups walnut pieces

Melt butter and add sugar. Beat in a bowl the eggs, vanilla and water. Add the butter/sugar mixture. Mix well.

Blend together the salt, baking powder, baking soda and whole wheat pastry flour. Mix dry and liquid ingredients together. Stir in coconut, wheat germ, chocolate chips and nuts.

Bake large cookies on a lightly greased cookie sheet at 350° for 12 to15 minutes.

Compliments of Jim Holloway, Wy'East Naturals

sweet ending

314

Chocolate Toll Bridge Cookies

makes 5 dozen

1 cup butter
1 cup brown sugar
2 eggs
1 tsp. vanilla
2 cups flour
2-1/2 cups oatmeal
1/2 tsp. salt
1 tsp. baking powder
1 tsp. baking soda
1-1/2 cups chopped nuts
12 ounces white chocolate chips*
4 ounce chocolate bar, grated

Cream together butter and sugar. Add eggs and vanilla. In blender or food processor, finely grind oatmeal to a flour consistency. Blend all dry ingredients together. Add to butter mixture. Stir in nuts and chocolates. Drop by tablespoons onto ungreased cookie sheets. Bake at 375° for 6 minutes.

* May substitute semi - sweet chocolate chips

Compliments of Betty Rea

s
w
e
e
t

e
n
d
i
n
g

==

Everyone will enjoy your wonderful Chocolate Toll Bridge Cookies while you picnic at Toll Bridge Park, located 2 miles south of the community of Mt. Hood, directly off Hwy. 35. The park opens April 1st each year and provides space for tent camping as well as R.V. hook-up, children's playground and covered facilities for group outings. A stone's throw away finds you on the banks of the East Fork of the Hood River.

Jam - Filled Cookies

makes 1 dozen

3/4 cup shortening
1/2 cup sugar
1/2 tsp. grated peel of orange, grapefruit or lemon
1 egg
2 cups flour
1/8 tsp. salt

jam or marmalade

Frosting:
3/4 cup powdered sugar
1/2 tsp. vanilla
milk

Cream shortening, sugar and peel. Add egg, mixing well. Add flour and salt, blending well. Adjust stiffness of dough by adding water or flour, to make it the right consistency for rolling out. Form into 2 balls and chill for 1 hour.

On lighlty floured surface, roll to 1/8-inch thick. Cut in rounds of desired size. Spread 1/2 of the number of rounds with jam (for extra eye-appeal, cut a small circle, square or heart from center of top round before putting in place). Place one round on top of another. Bake at 375° for 6 to 8 minutes. Cool on rack.

Combine frosting ingredients, adding enough milk for a spreadable consistency.

This recipe from Irene was reconstructed from her childhood memory of bakery cookies at the Baltic Sea.

Irene Aikin, Parkdale

s
w
e
e
t

e
n
d
i
n
g

316

Toffee Squares

1 cup butter
1 cup brown sugar
2 cups flour
1 egg yolk

1 tsp. vanilla
4 Hershey bars
chopped nuts

Cream butter and sugar. Add yolk, flour and vanilla. Spread in jelly roll pan, 1/4-inch thick.

Bake at 350° for 15 to 20 minutes, until brown. Place "Hershey" bars on hot cookie. When chocolate melts, spread to frost. Sprinkle with nuts.

This recipe is in memory of Margaret Madsen whose cookies were always delicious and beautiful. This is her son's favorite cookie.

Larry Madsen, Hood River

Spunky Biscuits

makes 48

2 cups flour
1 tsp. baking powder
1/4 tsp. baking soda
1 tsp. salt

2/3 cup butter
2 cups packed brown sugar
2 eggs, slightly beaten
2 tsp. vanilla
1 cup chocolate chips
1/3 cup chopped nuts

Mix first four ingredients. Set aside. Melt butter in saucepan; add sugar. Blend in eggs and vanilla. Add flour mixture gradually, blending well. Spread in a lightly buttered 9 x13-inch baking pan. Sprinkle with chocolate chips and nuts. Bake at 350° for 30 minutes. Cool in pan. Cut into bars.

JoAnn von Lubken, Hood River

MT. HOOD FRUIT CO.

McIsaac Family Farm Since 1905

Mt. Hood Fruit Company is located in the upper Hood River Valley and is owned and operated by the McIsaac family. They have taken their favorite variety of pears and apples and created a selection of gourmet dried fruit products. For that perfect gift or souvenir, try their specialties, which are chocolate dipped apples and pears, Mt. Snacks, and gift crates.

Mt. Hood Fruit Company makes their products available by mail order or through Wy'East Naturals, The Fruit Tree, McIsaac's Store and locally renowned craft fairs throughout the year.

Easy Pear Balls

1 6 ounce package dried pears, ground or finely
    cut up
2-1/2 cups flaked coconut
3/4 cup sweetened condensed milk
2/3 cup finely chopped nuts
powdered sugar

Mix all ingredients. Shape into 1-inch balls; roll in powdered sugar. Let stand 2 hours or until firm. Great to take along on hiking trips.

Compliments of Sandy McIsaac and Mt. Hood Fruit Company

s
w
e
e
t

e
n
d
i
n
g

318

Pride O'Scotland
Shortbread Wedges

2 cups flour
3/4 cup sugar
1/4 tsp. salt
1 cup butter, softened
1 egg yolk
1 tsp. vanilla

powdered sugar

Mix dry ingredients together. Add butter, egg yolk and vanilla. Mix with fingers until dough holds together. Divide the dough into two equal parts and, with floured palms, roll each into a ball. Press each ball into the bottom of a 9-inch pie pan. Flatten evenly and crimp edges as for pie crust. Prick surface with floured fork.

Bake at 375° for 20 to 25 minutes or until golden brown. Cut into 8 to 12 wedges. Dust with powdered sugar.

Pat McDonald, Hood River

s
w
e
e
t

e
n
d
i
n
g

Shortbread

3/4 cup sugar
1-1/2 cup butter
4 cups flour

Cream butter and sugar thoroughly. Add flour one cup at a time and mix well.

Press into a 9x15-inch jelly roll pan. Create a professional, festive look by stamping rows with a cookie stamp. Bake at 325° for 35 to 40 mintues. Cut into squares while hot.

Dough may also be rolled and cut with cookie cutter and stamped.

To create an absolutely scrumptious shortbread cookie, press the handle of a wooden spoon in a crisscross fashion and fill with raspberry or apricot jam and bake as usual. Remove from oven and drizzle powdered sugar glaze on baked jam. Perfection!

s
w
e
e
t

e
n
d
i
n
g

Lemon Sauce

1/2 cup sugar
1 Tb. cornstarch
1/8 tsp. salt
1/8 tsp. nutmeg
1 cup boiling water
2 Tb. butter
1-1/2 Tb. lemon juice

Mix sugar, cornstarch, salt and nutmeg together. Gradually add water and cook over low heat until thick. Add butter and lemon juice and stir until well blended. Serve warm or at room temperature.

Chocolate Sauce

2 squares of unsweetened chocolate
2 large Tb. butter
1 cup powdered sugar
4 Tb. milk or cream
1 egg
1 tsp. vanilla

Melt the chocolate and butter over hot water in a double boiler. Add powdered sugar and milk. Stir together.

In separate bowl, beat egg until frothy. Add to chocolate mixture and add vanilla. Simmer, stirring occasionally, about 20 minutes.

Recipe may be doubled or tripled.

Ruth Babson, Parkdale

321

Sweetened Condensed Milk

makes 2 cups

1-1/2 cups sugar
1/2 cup water
1/2 cup butter
1/2 tsp. vanilla
2 cups instant nonfat dry milk

Combine sugar, water and butter in dish suitable for a microwave. Bring to a full boil and cook for 3 to 4 minutes in microwave. Blend in vanilla and dry milk until smooth. Store in refrigerator. A great alternative for purchased sweetened condensed milk.

Bea Fischer, Mt. Hood

Gumjuwac Cracker Jacks

1/2 cup unpopped popcorn
1/2 cup sunflower seeds
1/2 cup unroasted peanuts
3 Tb. oil
1 cup molasses

Pop popcorn. Set aside in large bowl or paper sack. In frying pan, sauté seeds and peanuts in oil until lightly brown. Stir in molasses. Simmer until thick and bubbly. Pour mixture over popcorn, tossing gently. Eat and enjoy!

One hundred yards south of the Robinhood Campground entrance, turn east on the dirt road which leads to a parking area. The trail climbs steadily in a series of switchbacks for two miles to Gumjuwac Saddle where one can view Mt. Hood, the East Fork of Hood River, and Badger Creek Valley.

s
w
e
e
t

e
n
d
i
n
g

322

Index

323

328

331

* These recipes can be modified
to suit a vegetarian diet and
taste equally as delicious by
disregarding or substituting the
meat or poultry ingredient.

Notes

Notes

Mail to:

    Valley Collection...Gorge Connection
    P.O. Box 275
    Hood River, Oregon   97031

*Please send me_____copies of your cookbook at $16.95
per copy, plus $2.50 per copy for postage and handling.*

*Enclosed is my check or money order in the amount
of_____ (make checks payable to Valley Collection . . .
Gorge Connection)*

Name_____

Address_____

City_____State____Zip_____

I found out about your cookbook through_____

Gift card or personal message_____

Mail to:

    Valley Collection...Gorge Connection
    P.O. Box 275
    Hood River, Oregon   97031

*Please send me_____copies of your cookbook at $16.95
per copy, plus $2.50 per copy for postage and handling.*

*Enclosed is my check or money order in the amount
of_____ (make checks payable to Valley Collection . . .
Gorge Connection)*

Name_____

Address_____

City_____State____Zip_____

I found out about your cookbook through_____

Gift card or personal message_____

Mail to:
Valley Collection...Gorge Connection
P.O. Box 275
Hood River, Oregon   97031

Please send me_____copies of your cookbook at $16.95 per copy, plus $2.50 per copy for postage and handling.

Enclosed is my check or money order in the amount of_____ (make checks payable to Valley Collection ... Gorge Connection)

Name_____

Address_____

City_____State____Zip_____

I found out about your cookbook through_____

Gift card or personal message_____

Mail to:
Valley Collection...Gorge Connection
P.O. Box 275
Hood River, Oregon   97031

Please send me_____copies of your cookbook at $16.95 per copy, plus $2.50 per copy for postage and handling.

Enclosed is my check or money order in the amount of_____ (make checks payable to Valley Collection ... Gorge Connection)

Name_____

Address_____

City_____State____Zip_____

I found out about your cookbook through_____

Gift card or personal message_____